Sunday Morning
MEMORIES

Sunday Morning
MEMORIES

A Humorous and Inspirational Look at Growing up in the Church

Don Reid

New Leaf Press

To
Sidney and Frances, my mom and dad

and

Harold and Faye, my brother and sister

They were there
And always are

Contents

Foreword

H e's my little brother." That's what I thought when he called and asked me if I'd read his book and write a foreword.

So, let's start at the beginning. When I was a very comfortable and happy six year old, my mother came home after being gone a couple of days with something they call a little brother. Now let's be honest. I wasn't exactly thrilled about this bundle of boy. I had not volunteered nor been asked to start sharing toys, time, or a mother. I was already burdened with the dreaded older sister, so I didn't need more stress.

But after several days (seemed like months), Mom and Dad convinced me that we would not be returning him to the hospital. That was my first big lesson in life. Sometimes there just ain't nothin' you can do. You'd better make the best of it.

So I started my lifelong journey to teach him everything I knew. That took a little less than seven minutes, but we were forever best friends. I taught him how to play ball, but he figured out how to hit safely every time he'd bat. I drug him to cowboy movies on Saturday mornings, but he was the one who discovered classic drama. Of course, I took him to school with me on the last day before summer vacation to show him off, because he was, after all, my little brother.

Then we started singing in a little quartet together and he began to grow and learn and write songs way beyond his years, and sometimes I felt like the little brother. He's never learned as much from me as I have from him.

So now I've read his book. I'm not surprised; you might be, but I'm not. He can plant a word and grow a tear. He'll inspire you and make you laugh, then entertain you and make you cry. These stories are special. They're real and, best of all, they're true. Every one of them. I know, because I was there.

You know the people in this book or some just like them. You've been to this church or meeting hall or social event. And you'll recognize friends, family, and yourself. These are precious memories. You're gonna have a good time. Why, you ask?

Because it's good. It's well written. It's honest. And, after all, he's my little brother.

— Harold Reid
His biggest brother
His biggest fan

PRECIOUS MEMORIES, HOW THEY LINGER!
HOW THEY EVER FLOOD MY SOUL!
IN THE STILLNESS OF THE MIDNIGHT,
PRECIOUS SACRED SCENES UNFOLD.

Preface

I do my best writing not at the computer or at my desk with a pad and pencil, but standing in the backyard throwing a tennis ball to my dog, Chipper.

We spend countless hours each week, me bouncing the tennis ball and him catching it on the second or third bounce and bringing it back and laying it at my feet. That's where my mind is free and starts to accumulate ideas and form words and paragraphs to be set down later in print.

I write songs and poems and Sunday school lessons and books in my head till his legs get tired or my arm gives out, whichever comes first, and then we go inside and I put it all together while he sleeps under my desk in wait for the next ball game.

SUNDAY MORNING MEMORIES came just this way. I thought about the stories I wanted to tell and realized, way before the title came, just how much of my life had been centered round the church. I grew up with the church building itself and the church people being such an integral part of my daily life. Sunday morning services, Sunday school, weddings, funerals, vacation Bible school, picnics, ballgames, Halloween parties, Christmas pageants, covered-dish suppers. All at the church. As a kid, I lived just down the road, and it seems we were there every other day for something.

I had a friend once who was just as big a movie fan as I have always been and he always said he got most of his education at the movies. I did, too. We never learned in school exactly where Casablanca was. But we found out at the movies. *The Best Years of Our Lives* and *Battle Cry* taught me more about WWII than any sixth grade history class ever did. *Red Planet Mars* and *Conquest of Space* did more to pique my preteen interest than Mr. Baker's science lab ever did. And *Ben-Hur* and *The Greatest Story Ever Told* and *Samson and Delilah*, well, need I go on? I've often thought that if I could have spent a few more days at church and at the movies, I wouldn't have had to go to school.

Now I may take a few sideways glances in these pages at my denomination and some of our ways, but all in good faith and fun. I may offer a few tongue-in-cheek opinions and an occasional wink at some rules and rituals, but it's all good-hearted and well-intentioned. All the memories in these pages are from my church experiences if not actually from Sunday *mornings.* I learned a lot about life and good people and who I was and who I wanted to be from those times and am still learning them. Every Sunday morning. And I'm reliving them with every passing day. With every fading memory. With every bounce of the ball.

I've got to go now. Chipper wants to play.

Attendance

Getting up and going to church on Sunday mornings can become a habit the same as staying in bed and reading the paper on Sunday mornings can become a habit. A habit is something you do without thinking; something you do without a lot of effort; something you feel guilty about if you don't do it. Ask any regular churchgoer and he/she will tell you that on the Sundays they don't go, their whole week is upside-down. Mondays feel like Wednesdays. Thursdays feel like Fridays. And that Sunday feels like a Saturday.

On my way to church every Lord's Day morning (notice I didn't say Sabbath — I know we Presbyterians don't remember the Sabbath and keep it holy), I always have to drive through town to pick up my mother. On my way, I see sights you would expect to see any of the other six days of the weeks. At 9:30 a.m., people are mowing their yards, weeding their flowerbeds, and cleaning their gutters. On down into the heart of the commercial part of town, there is hardly a summer Sunday morning you don't see an office building being painted or a parking lot being re-lined, or a driveway being hosed, or a plate glass window being squeegeed. Sunday mornings are just not important to everyone or maybe they have just never developed *the habit*.

On the other hand, once you get to church, there are people there who will be there in spite of rain, hail, sleet, flood, or sickness. Only death can keep them away and then only *their* death. When I was a kid, our Sunday school department used to give out attendance pins. I think they started with three months of perfect attendance and then went to six months and a year. And then with each year thereafter, you got a little attachment that hung down and hooked on the one above it and if you wore it on your coat lapel, after about five years, you looked like a member of some Middle-Eastern army. We had one older gentleman, Mr. Kyle Foster, who had a string of gold

18

attachments that reached almost to his waist and he would change it from coat to coat each Sunday morning. He was regular and proud of it. He had *the habit.*

I recently read an article on the U.S. Presidents and their religions. It told what denomination each was and their church-going habits. I was surprised to find that not all of them had *the habit.* Three had no church affiliation at all. Never attended with any regularity in or out of office. And the number three was not so much the shocker as to who they were.

One was Andrew Johnson. I think he was brought up on impeachment charges after the Civil War if my high school history memories don't fail me. He doesn't surprise me much.

Another was my fellow state-mate, Thomas Jefferson. This doesn't surprise me as much as it disappoints me. Author of the Declaration of Independence. Father of the University of Virginia. Congressman. Secretary of state. Vice president. And finally president. And yet he couldn't find time to go to church every once in awhile.

And the third was our saintly 16th, ole Honest Abe himself. America has done everything but give him wings and a halo, but Abe wanted no part of it. Sunday morning worship service and church membership was not on his weekly agenda.

Of course, I realize that none of us are going to be judged on how many pews we filled and how often we filled them. What we got out of the experience and how we used it is what is going to count in the long run.

Seeing the same faces every Sunday is a comfort to me. And even when I visit other churches, I still see the same faces. I identify them with the ones I know from my home church. Church people and congregations are the same all over the country. They have the same hearts and the same purpose. They have the same goal and the same concerns. They have the same spirit and the same God.

They have the same *habit*.

COME TO THE CHURCH IN THE WILDWOOD,
O COME TO THE CHURCH IN THE DALE.
NO SPOT IS SO DEAR TO MY CHILDHOOD
AS THE LITTLE BROWN CHURCH IN THE VALE.

Baptism

John made quite a name for himself baptizing people in the Jordan River. He served so many, he earned the name "The Baptizer." He would hold them at their back with one hand and put his other hand on their forehead and ease them over until they were completely submersed, and then say the words over them that would prepare them for a God-fearing life on earth and heaven. But of all the many people John baptized, and

I know Jesus was one, there is no record in all biblical history that any of them was a Presbyterian.

Stand in a cold, murky river fully dressed and let someone bend you over backward and run water up your nose? It has never as much as crossed our minds. And what kind of shoes are they wearing down there? Barefooted maybe with river mud squishing between their toes? No, thank you. We don't wade. Even when we fish, Presbyterians sit on the bank with a long line.

Our baptizing is a very simple sacrament. No great planning goes into it. You don't have to book it weeks in advance so that you and the preacher can wear your old clothes that morning or wait till spring for the water to warm up and have everyone meet down at the river after the service. You don't have to put on a robe or towel dry your hair in public and you don't have to fear coughing up water in front of a hundred and fifty people. It's very simple with us.

We just walk up front and the minister dips his fingers in a sliver cup and dabs a little bit of water on our heads while we cringe and fear that he's going to mess up a hairdo it took all morning to fix, comb, or curl. Then he'll say a few words over us and we're back in our seats and ready for our nap before you can say "heavenly dove."

We can do four, five, six, seven; however many you want right in a row and never cause a problem or a puddle. We do babies, old ladies, teenagers, newcomers, and latecomers. We

22

don't care. Everybody gets the same treatment. John baptized with water. Jesus baptized with the Holy Spirit. But Presbyterians baptize with comfort. No wrinkles. No mess. And it's just as good as anybody else can offer.

Baptizing in the river? Full submersion? Not for us. We'll take a little sprinkling and that will do us just fine, thank you. My wife is a Baptist and she's been promising for years to take me along to the river some summer Sunday to watch it all done as only the Southern Baptists can do it. I've made her the same offer, to take her with me to watch how we do it, but her only reaction is, "What's to see?"

Things happen. Babies squirm. Elders spill water. Preachers forget the subject's name. And babies squirm. And sometimes yell to the top of their voices and to the ends of our nerves. But no matter what church you're in, when it's all over and your clothes are dried and our hairdos are fluffed, we're all baptized. We all have personally and publicly become a member of the body of Christ. In the name of the Father, and the Son, and the Holy Ghost.

YES, WE'LL GATHER AT THE RIVER,
THE BEAUTIFUL, THE BEAUTIFUL RIVER.
GATHER WITH THE SAINTS AT THE RIVER
THAT FLOWS BY THE THRONE OF GOD.

Boy Scout Troop 34

O f course, it wasn't on Sunday mornings. It was on Wednesday nights. But it was in the church. In the basement of the church next to the furnace room where it was so hot in the winter months that when we had to raise the window to have our meetings, the snow would blow in. Our faces would freeze and our feet would burn up, but we were Boy Scouts and we could take it. We were Presbyterian-sponsored Boy Scouts and we had uniforms and merit badges and we knew the motto, the oath and the law. "Be Prepared." That was the first and easiest thing to learn. And the oath. "On my honor I will do my best to do my duty to God and my country . . ." and on and on.

And do you really think I've forgotten the 12 points of the Scout Law? No way. "A Boy Scout is trustworthy, loyal, helpful, friendly, courteous, kind, obedient, cheerful, thrifty, brave, clean, and reverent."

All of this knowledge and an overnight camping trip would get you your first rank. Your Tenderfoot pin. And I wore it with pride on my army-green uniform. Left pocket, over my heart. It was easy. Although the overnight camping trip was a little harder.

All of our scoutmasters were elders in our church. So when those mandatory camping trips came up, they had to take us whether they liked it or not. They not only had the Boy Scouts USA watching them, they had the church session looking over their shoulders.

The first outing was a simple afternoon hike that went into suppertime and got us home after dark. On this one I learned to cook. I fried eggs in my miniature skillet and drank warm, flat Pepsi out of my army canteen. I was on my way to being a woodsman of the world.

The next one was a little bigger deal. We went on a weekend camping Jamboree, pitched our own tents and un-furled our own sleeping bags, and lay there in our temporary canvas homes while it rained torrents all night long and mud seeped in around our bedding and into our clothes like chocolate syrup on a banana split. Cold and miserable and wanting to go home, my tentmate and I crawled out of the flap about 3 a.m. and went to the scoutmaster's/elder's tent for some relief. We found him asleep in a luxurious Big Top, on an army bed, high on a wooden platform that defied any gulches of water that might run through. He offered one of his woolen blankets and let us sleep on the wooden platform the rest of the night. I realized then that I would probably never get past my Tenderfoot pin, and more importantly, that I would never really want to. I tend to prefer dry, warm, and smooth instead of their opposites.

27

But that's not what got me out of scouting or what got scouting out of the church. I stayed around long enough to get my Second Class pin and a few easy merit badges. I marched in a couple of parades, tied a few knots, and was even given the troop bugle to learn to blow Taps and Reveille. (I was in the grade school band and played alto saxophone, so they thought I would be a natural on the bugle. Only a musician will know that that is like thinking if you can play ping pong, you can bowl.) What finally got me out of the Scouts was an injury. Not a scout-related injury even. Nothing as honorable as an insect bite or getting lost in the woods and losing blood from the branches that scratched my face. Nothing like that. We were playing football on the church lawn before a troop meeting one

Wednesday night and somebody tackled me and broke my ankle. Two other elders, who were also scoutmasters or helpers, drove me home and one carried me up the front steps on his shoulders and I remember the porch light coming on and Mama opening the door and the look on her face when she saw me. From that day on, I pretty much had it with the Scouts and football. I didn't have to sleep in wet tents and eat my own fried eggs anymore. Didn't have to march in Christmas parades till my nose was numb and red. And I didn't have to wear my uniform to school one day a week. (Fridays, if I remember correctly.)

Not long after that, the church got out of the Scouting business. Certainly not because of me getting injured. But probably because it takes special men to donate and dedicate that kind of time to such a noble organization. And it takes special boys to want to learn and be and do and achieve all that the Scouts demand. It was a time when God was a visible part of the program. He wasn't hid and ignored. He was right there in the oath. Not downplayed. And it was a church-sponsored event. Taking young boys and teaching them a little religion and a little life and proud to do it.

TAKE MY LIFE, AND LET IT BE
CONSECRATED, LORD TO THEE.
TAKE MY MOMENTS AND MY DAYS,
LET THEM FLOW IN CEASELESS PRAISE.
LET THEM FLOW IN CEASLEESS PRAISE.

Candlelight Service

This service is partially misnamed. The whole thing isn't candlelit, only the last few minutes. And a few minutes of terror they can be.

Here's the way most of them work. In our church, the lights are normal to low for most of the worship service and then turned completely off at the end and everyone picks up a candle that you have been given when you came in and a couple of elders pass down the aisle and light you up. Now the trick is, and very explicit instructions are given, that the elder will hold his candle with the flame straight up and the person on the end of the aisle will tilt theirs to get a flame from his. Then you pass it on the same way. But never, never tilt the candle with the flame or hot wax will run down your hand and you may yell out something you don't want your mother to hear. This works most of the time. Of course, one time is all it takes. That dried wax is hard to get off dresses, suit pants, carpet, and skin.

Now up the road at the Baptist church, my wife's place of worship, they do the same thing but with a little different twist. They don't have elders, so to show us how inept our governing body is, they have pre-school children doing the same duty. Pound for pound and candle for candle, the kids spill less wax every year than our astute elders. If you're keeping score that's 1 for the Baptists — 0 for the Presbyterians.

Debbie and I always go to both candlelight services on Christmas Eve. It's become a tradition with us. Thank goodness, the hours of the services allow us to get to both on time. It has become one of the most important parts of our Christmas season. And it's not how different they are that fascinates me but how similar they are.

If I may get personal for a moment, we have a wonderful minister known to the entire congregation as Joe. Little kids and old people alike simply call him Joe and this seems to be fine with him. And every year, after everyone gets seated, he looks us all in the eye from the pulpit and says something to the nature of, "This is it. The stores have closed. The rush is over. It's time to take a deep breath and relax. If you haven't done it by now, it's not going to get done," and then puts us all in a spiritual state we haven't been able to capture all season. It's peaceful and soothing and casual and you can't help but feel the true meaning of Christmas in every muscle and nerve in your body.

Then we go to Debbie's church, and, believe it or not, she has a minister whose first name is Temple and little kids and old people alike simply call him Temple and this seems to be fine with him, too. For about 45 minutes, they have a talent program that all ages participate in and we all applaud after each song and then the lights go down low and Temple says something to the nature of, "From here on, we won't applaud. From here on this is a worship service." And he also puts us in a mood that can only be felt on a Christmas Eve night. Peaceful and in touch with God and ourselves.

Both of these men are religious heroes to me, and the love and respect they have for their congregations can only be surpassed by the reciprocal love and respect their congregations have for them. They have reinvented the spirit of Christmas Eve and defined it in terms that everyone should experience.

I always go home a little better person by having been there. And I always find myself, no matter how cold, standing outside before the night is over and looking for the star and thanking God for His gift. And then thanking God for Joe and

Temple and Mama and Daddy and my wife and sons; everyone who makes Christmas for me such a special, happy, and religious season.

> SILENT NIGHT, HOLY NIGHT,
> ALL IS CALM, ALL IS BRIGHT.
> ROUND YON VIRGIN, MOTHER AND CHILD,
> HOLY INFANT SO TENDER AND MILD,
> SLEEP IN HEAVENLY PEACE;
> SLEEP IN HEAVENLY PEACE.

The Children's Sermon

A separate and special sermon for the children of the congregation is a relatively new idea in church life. New to me anyway. We never had one when I was growing up. No nursery, as I have noted elsewhere, and no break from the formality of the morning worship service with little trips up to the front and sitting around on the floor in your good clothes. Sitting on the floor in church when I was a kid could not only get you frowned at, it could possibly get your arm jerked.

I was only aware of the existence of a children's message about 30 years ago. This may have been when they first got popular on a national scale, or it may have just been when we first started doing it. In our part of the country we always get things late. We didn't know about hula hoops until the late sixties and we didn't know Elvis was dead until somebody spotted him at a local 7-11. We just thought he was passing through town.

But upon its arrival, the Children's Sermon, and I spell it this way because it now has its own place in the bulletin, took on a life of its own. All congregations have their own style in instructing the young. Some direct them to a side door at a particular point in the service and they exit and have their lesson somewhere in a nearby room. Others have the children come down the aisle and sit up front while the minister gets down with them and tells them a philosophical or biblical story on their level of understanding. While still others, and this is the way we do it, have random adult members meet the kids on the floor in front of the pulpit, sit on the carpeted steps and do battle with one another. This latter method carries a number of negatives that I'm going to share with you now so that when and if it comes up at your church you can vote on the one where the preacher does it every Sunday.

Every year, a couple of new elders are arm-twisted into heading up the Children's Sermon committee. This means they have to seek out 52 willing members to hold court with the kids each Sunday morning. And each year it's fun to watch those two poor souls walking the halls of the church and seeing people ducking into Sunday school rooms and hiding in coat closets to keep from being buttonholed.

But the list is finally put together and added to each week, and a few guidelines are offered to those who are unlucky enough to be found among the coats.

Number one — keep it to three minutes. Why, some may ask? Easy question. These are children, and their attention spans are not fully developed and it is vitally important to keep it simple, short, and to the point. Short should not be hard, but it tends to be the most difficult point for the adults to adhere to. Simple should be even easier and yet you will hear six syllable words flying like dust in the sunlight. And to the point is the easiest of all if indeed you have a point.

Number two — make statements. Don't ask questions. Don't ask a four or five year old, "What did you do this week?" or "Do you like to go to school?" Once a four or five year old has the floor and gets a few laughs, you'll never get back on track. And look at your watch. Six minutes have already gone by and you haven't even got to your closing poem or however you're planning on finishing.

And number three — talk to the kids. You don't need a microphone. The children are right at your feet. Talk to the kids. Don't pick a subject or punchline that only the congregation will understand. It's the Children's Sermon.

I think I'll quit with that as I have probably offended enough people with just three points. Should I go on to my planned ten, we'd never get anyone to say yes again.

But seriously, folks, and I haven't been serious up until now, I have the most sincere love and respect for anyone who takes their time to do anything for a child. Jesus set the perfect example. His disciples gave the parents a bad time when they tried to get their children close to Him where they could touch Him and be touched by Him. But Jesus saw what was happening and stopped them and said, "Let the little children come to me. Anyone who does not accept God with the simplicity of a child will never see heaven."

So let's keep those Children's Sermons coming. No matter how much arm-twisting we have to do and no matter how many times someone says, "I don't know what to talk about. Get someone else." Stay after them for the children's sake. I think Jesus would want it that way.

JESUS LOVES ME THIS I KNOW,
FOR THE BIBLE TELLS ME SO.
LITTLE ONES TO HIM BELONG;
THEY ARE WEAK BUT HE IS STRONG.

YES, JESUS LOVES ME!
YES, JESUS LOVES ME!
YES, JESUS LOVES ME!
FOR THE BIBLE TELLS ME SO .

The Choir

The choir is always the best or the worst seat in the house. If you're sitting behind the preacher or on one side or the other of him, it's the worst. You're looking at all the congregation, right straight in the eye for 60 minutes. Oh, you know who's dozing and who's whispering and who's chewing gum, but they also can see whatever it is you may be doing. Unless, of course, you're a "professional" choir singer. What's the difference, you ask, between a professional choir singer and an amateur? Very simple. It's the look on their faces during the sermon.

A professional choir singer can make the look of boredom appear to be rapture. A professional can make that faraway look in their eye that comes from their mind wandering from what they did last night to what they're going to do Monday morning, look like engulfed interest and concern. A true choir professional can fool all the congregants all the time. A good and experienced choir professional can even close his or her eyes and get a short nap if they keep their chin elevated and their hand under it for support. But if you're lucky enough to have one of those churches where the choir is in the balcony behind the congregation facing the preacher, then you have the best seat. The only person who's looking at you then is the preacher and he's got a hundred or so others to keep his eye on, which lets you considerably off the hook.

If you're careful and on your toes even just a little, you can leaf through a catalog or jot down some reminders for next week, file your nails, sew, whisper to your neighbor, pass notes, and even eat candy after the anthem. You can for sure take your shoes off between songs and, if necessary and if not necessary, get up and walk out for a break without disturbing anyone or being noticed by anyone. You can unzip your robe on hot mornings and fan yourself. And you can daydream with a clear conscience with no fear of anyone seeing it on your face.

38

The only drawback to the "balcony choir" is that it seldom ever produces a true and good choir professional. There is just no motivation.

I loved watching the choir when I was a kid. I loved watching them march in and down the aisle with their long, flowing, dark blue robes, swishing by the pews and up the steps to the choir loft. And when they got to their seats, they were always in perfect order. The sopranos were all together, the altos, the tenors, the basses. The women on the front rows, the men on the back. And what fascinated me most was how they could walk and sing at the same time and never miss a note or a word. And speaking of words, the really coolest thing was when I'd look up and see them singing a hymn without looking at the book. I loved it when they knew a hymn by heart and marveled when we sang a new one and knew that they could read the words and the music at the same time and still never miss a note or a syllable. That choir thing was as close to church celebrity as being an usher. And I sorely wanted to be both.

We've had a number of different organists with the choir. All of them have been pretty good, and the one we have now and have had for years, is off the scale somewhere above excellent. I remember one when I was a kid, who used to ride his bicycle to church, park it by the tree on the front lawn, go in and play the organ, and then come out and tie a string around the right leg of his pants on his blue serge suit and ride his bike home as if it were the most natural thing a 35-year-old man ever did.

I don't remember if he was any good or not. The only thing I remember was the 26-inch Schwinn with the chrome handlebars. One thing that took my mind off the sermons at that age, and there were many things, but one was the organist's feet. We had a big fancy organ with the foot pedals. The feet on the pedals that she never looked at were as much a mystery to me as watching Daddy's feet on the clutch and brake and accelerator in the car. How did they know where to put them? She (we had a woman by this time) would watch the music and never her hands and never her feet, and still turn the pages and never hit a sour note and just completely hypnotize me with her every move. A pump organ I could understand, and those three little things under a piano looked like no problem at all, but I'm still in awe of the foot pedals on the organ. It may take long fingers to play a guitar, but it takes a lady of some length to play the pedals. A short woman could never reach that bass pedal on the far left but then she could never push the clutch in all the way either, could she? Which might explain why that first guy rode a bike.

There's been some scandal in the choir. In all choirs. They're a pretty close-knit group, and anytime you have a close group, there's scandal. People fall out and fall in with others. Gossip ensues. Feelings get hurt. Things get patched up and the Christmas cantata must go on. I was never privy to the inside of any of those little shakeups, but I remember one that got around that actually brought the choir members closer together. It was the routine that every Sunday morning in the choir room, in the basement of the church where the members put on their robes, the ladies would pile their purses in a corner, hang their coats on hooks, and march to the sanctuary. But then after the service, some of the women found things missing from their pocketbooks. Things like money. Somebody was apparently coming in from the street and stealing from the choir members during the church service. So even after locks were installed on the choir room door, the women would march down the aisle with hymnbook in hand, with their Sunday purses hanging on their arms. It takes a while for a Presbyterian stung to regain trust in even a locked door.

Sometimes they'd fall out over the type of anthems that should be sung. Some favored the new arrangements that present a challenge to sing, to the old favorites that had been on file for decades. Every January found a few members sitting in the congregation who had vowed to take a rest from the weekly grind of choir practice on Thursday night and the Sunday morning routine. This would last only a couple of months and by Easter the choir would be back to its original size with all the familiar faces intact.

I have the greatest respect for the church choir and its every musical member. They rehearse and practice and review with the sincerest dedication. They perform the every-Sunday duties and all the special music of the Easter and Christmas seasons. They review each hymn that is to be sung Sunday mornings so they'll know them even if the congregation doesn't. And they do all this with no fanfare whatsoever. And that is the one big rub I have about church choirs. So many times after a particularly moving anthem or solo, I have wanted to show my appreciation with applause. This is a sanctified no-no but is loosening up a little with each passing year. One of these mornings I'm going to stand up, applaud, and yell, "Do it again!"

And then the choir, whether they have the best seats or the worst seats in the house, will know just how much they're appreciated. And then I'm going to yell, "Let's hear it for the organist's feet!"

That's where the real talent is.

SING THEM OVER AGAIN TO ME,
WONDERFUL WORDS OF LIFE;
LET ME MORE OF THEIR BEAUTY SEE,
WONDERFUL WORDS OF LIFE.
WORDS OF LIFE AND BEAUTY,
TEACH ME FAITH AND DUTY:
BEAUTIFUL WORDS, WONDERFUL WORDS,
WONDERFUL WORDS OF LIFE.
BEAUTIFUL WORDS, WONDERFUL WORDS,
WONDERFUL WORDS OF LIFE.

The Christmas Pageant

If you've ever heard anyone say, "Christmas is for children," they were probably referring to Santa Claus and giving gifts and Christmas morning and the tree and the lights and all the trappings that go with a red and green holiday celebration. And maybe that's true. But to be real honest, I've never tired of it even as an adult. I still love it just as much as I ever did. I look forward to it. I like the bustle and the crowds and the scheming and the shopping and the decorations.

I like the fever and the energy and the dinners and the get-togethers and the music. I like the colors everyone wears and the looks on their faces and walking down the street and strangers saying "Merry Christmas" to one another. There's nothing I don't like about it.

And if you've ever heard anyone at church say, "Christmas is for children," what they probably mean is the Christmas Pageant. I have seen it presented both ways. I can remember years when the adults put on the play. Teenage boys playing shepherds and men playing wise men with a middle-aged Mary and Joseph. And even a real baby in the manger. These plays were slick and effective but uneventful.

The best ones were always the ones with the little folks. The five, six, and seven year olds. Little shepherds and slightly taller wise men. A Mary who would bring her doll baby and lay him in the hay and a Joseph who would prance and wave at his parents from the stage. And they all usually needed hands-on direction and would have to be turned and pointed to their next mark. These are the ones people remember. And the crowds are always bigger for these spectaculars. Not only parents in the audience, but grandparents and aunts and uncles and cousins from other churches and some who would never come inside a church for any other reason. This is why Christmas is for children.

And my hat is off to the women, as it always seems to be the women, because they have more patience, who direct these kids and practice these kids and make it special for them and for all of us.

As a young, over-principled, near adult, I remember taking issue with our minister over a Christmas program many years ago because after the Nativity scene, the curtain closed and St. Nick came out in his bright red suit with a pack on his back and gave oranges to all the kids. I thought this was mixing it up way too much. I felt there was no room for both in a church program. I'm older now and a wee bit wiser and concede that whatever it takes to get kids in church is pretty much all right with me. Mixing the Christmas myths with the Christmas facts is still a little awkward for me, but I do it on a personal basis and we shouldn't be ashamed to do anything at church that we do at home.

I treasure the Christmas pageants I was in as a child. The prettiest little girl was always Mary and the most popular boy was always Joseph. I was never even a wise man. It seems I was always a shepherd and sometimes there were four of us and sometimes six. Just whatever was left over. They'd give us a robe and headgear, a staff and some cardboard sandals and we were as happy as if we really knew what we were doing. But it was Christmas and we all knew that that spotlight over the manger was the focal point and we were just players. And thereby lay the lesson.

Christmas without a children's pageant is like a song without a melody.

AWAY IN A MANGER,
NO CRIB FOR A BED,
THE LITTLE LORD JESUS
LAY DOWN HIS SWEET HEAD.
THE STARS IN THE SKY
LOOK DOWN WHERE HE LAY,
THE LITTLE LORD JESUS
ALSEEP ON THE HAY.

Communion

Some churches serve wine. Some grape juice. Some churches break the bread. Some already have it broken.

Some churches believe the wine actually turns into the blood of Jesus.

Some believe the bread turns into His body.

As for me, I'm a Presbyterian.

We don't walk up the aisle and receive the bread. We'll just sit here in the pew and let you bring it to us. We don't stand in line to drink of the cup. Bring that on back here after you put the bread away. And we don't hold the bread or the wine in our hands until everyone is served and then partake of it together. When we get it, we eat it. When the drink comes, we drink it. We're Presbyterians and we don't have time for a lot of ceremony. (We also believe in predestination so that we don't have to make any decisions.)

I found myself at the front door of a hotel in upstate New York one Sunday morning, dressed in suit and tie, and ready to go to church. The doorman told me there was an Episcopalian church "right there across the street," a Methodist "a block up the street," and a Presbyterian "two blocks down." So like the lazy Christian I am, I went the Episcopal route because it was "right there across the street."

That's a little unfair. I went because I had never been to one. I was curious. I was hungry for a new experience. I wanted to broaden my scope. And it was "right there across the street."

It was an enormous and beautiful old church. The pews were from another century with dark wood and high backs. You sort of felt like you were in an expensive restaurant instead of a church and didn't know whether to ask for a bulletin or a menu.

There was a cushioned kneeling bar at your feet all the way across the back of the pew. Some knelt as they entered, as the Catholics do, and some didn't. It was apparently optional, and I didn't. Flags and banners hung from the high ceiling, down the center aisle. And I was strangely aware of people entering at all points during the service. They came in during the morning announcements. During the singing of the hymns. During the sermon. Except during prayer, they came in whenever they arrived or wanted to. It was a very formal setting with a very loose atmosphere. And the dress supported this also. I saw suits and ties and high heels and I saw jeans and t-shirts and tennis shoes. I felt both over and underdressed at the same time.

A sign out front announced the Morning Worship Service and Children's School, both at 10:30 a.m. And sure enough, after the first ten minutes of the service, the minister excused all the children, and everyone under the age of about 14 years got up and left through a side door and never came back. It was like stepping into a Stephen King novel. "Where have all the children gone and when are they coming back?"

But I race ahead. To begin the service, the organist played a dramatic warm-up of music for five minutes and then hit an apex and the congregation stood and the choir marched in carrying flags and songbooks and singing to the top of their voices. They looked like they were coming to do battle. A flourish of colored flags and old English music. They entered from the front left corner and marched down that aisle to the back of the church and then up the center aisle, then up the right aisle and back down the center again. I couldn't tell if they were lost or just enjoying themselves.

Once the choir got settled, we had prayers from our prayer books and the pastor entered in an elegant robe and even walked the aisles while he made the morning announcements. It was all very friendly and the sermon that followed was very good. He talked about Lazarus and tied it in with the Old Testament Scripture about the dry bones that got up and walked around. Very good and very clever.

Then just as things were winding down, or I thought they were, an assistant minister appeared and took over. He was an older gentleman who looked unfamiliar, but who talked exactly like Michael Caine. And this was rather distracting as I was constantly waiting for the punch line. It was like a "Saturday Night Live" skit. Michael Caine as the priest and I'm sitting on the next to last row, so his facial features are not very pronounced and it all began to take on a surreal feeling. And it actually crossed my mind that there was no way, from this distance, to be sure it wasn't Michael Caine.

But before this notion had time to take root, the Rev. Caine turned his back to the congregation and began reading long and hard from a big book, directly into the wall behind the pulpit. He had a microphone, so I could still hear him. And so could all the city because it said right there in the bulletin that the service was being carried on 1360 AM. And his purpose in doing this was to prepare us all for Holy Communion. The Eucharist.

And then it began. The first reverend handed out bread to the choir and the second reverend picked up a tall gold chalice and passed in front of each choir member and they sipped from it. After each sip, Rev. Caine took his white handkerchief and wiped the brim of the cup, then stepped to the next one.

My eyes went from the handkerchief slowly to the front door. Just how many steps would it be from my pew to the sunlight on the other side of those double doors?

Two ushers walked down the center aisle to let the first row out the way you've all seen it done at weddings and funerals. With each row they stepped closer toward the back as each row heading toward the front took a piece of bread and drank from that one, lone, gold cup. I watched all this from my vantage point on the second row from the back and the only thing I was seeing was that white handkerchief brushing across the rim of that cup. The ushers were getting closer and that front door was looking farther away. Dare I make a run for it? Dare I stay and drink? You're looking at a man who carries antiseptic towelettes in his pocket to use after shaking hands with people. Would it be irreverent to leave at this point?

My head was swirling and my heart was pounding as the ushers got as close to me as the front door was behind me. It was equal ground. I could stay and take my chances on the handkerchief or I could make a dash for the front door and no one would ever know who I was. My final decision was *Homey don't do no one-cup drinking. Homey don't play that game.* I got up as reverently and as quietly as possible and walked out the front door. It was like the glossolalia (see page 91). There's nothing wrong with it if you're used to that, but I'm Presbyterian and we're not used to anything.

> BREAK THOU THE BREAD OF LIFE,
> DEAR LORD, TO ME,
> AS THOU DID BREAK THE LOAVES
> BESIDE THE SEA;
> BEYOND THE SACRED PAGE
> I SEEK THEE LORD;
> MY SPIRIT PANTS FOR THEE,
> O LIVING WORD.

Covered Dish Suppers

Maybe you call them something else at your church, but you know what I'm talking about. Everybody brings a dish: a casserole, a salad, meat, or potatoes. You put them on a big, long table and everyone goes around and fills their plates with four different kinds of macaroni and cheese and anything else that might catch the eye, and then you eat till you can't possibly eat any more, and when you're completely and unreservedly stuffed, you go to the dessert table. Pies: chocolate, butterscotch, lemon, and apple. Cakes: chocolate, coconut, German chocolate, and carrot. You fill your plate with more desserts than you normally eat in a month and go back and sit down and eat and complain about how full you are as if someone has been holding a .38 caliber pistol to your head.

The women clean up the kitchen and the social hall, and the dishes, with their glass tops and plastic lids and silver carrying handles, are toted home and washed and readied for the next "church supper."

I've been to hundreds of them. As a kid I looked forward to them. It was a night out. A time to run around the church grounds with other kids and do silly and memorable things together. And when the time came to eat, we'd all be called and the minister would say grace and bless the food and all the hands that had prepared it and then we'd rush for the front of the line and our parents would grab us and make us wait till some of the older people went first. When we finally did get in line, there was always plenty left even though we feared there wouldn't be. We looked every dish over with care and searched for what our mothers brought and took full advantage of the sovereignty of filling our own plates by not taking on anything green or leafy. If it didn't have cheese or chocolate in it, we pretty much skipped it.

There were always stories that lasted through the years of those "family night suppers." My wife remembers the time her daddy got in the car, heading for a church dinner, and threw his dress hat in the back seat and it landed, brim-first, in a meringue pie. She also remembers her cousin putting a large dish of baked beans in the trunk of her car and by the time it arrived at the church parking lot, the dish was empty but the trunk wasn't. What a mess!

I have no memories such as these to blame my absence from current dinners on. I started shying away from "potluck suppers" for two different reasons. One was the food, but the other was the program that followed. Usually someone would bring a slide projector and, friend, when someone pulls out a slide machine of any kind, be it in their home, at a party, or at church, take advice from one who knows and RUN. It may be a missionary who has been in the "field" for years and dedicated his life and is there to raise money for future ventures. I'm all for it. Give him the money, but you can only look at so many thatched-roof huts in an hour and a half, and that was the length of the last one I sat through. When it was over, I vowed off, not the giving, but the attending. More effect can come from a 15-minute presentation than from a 90-minute one. Six times as long does not mean six times as good.

It may be a preacher from another county who took a trip to the Holy Land and his briefcase full of slides is his opening to the Suppertime Speaking Tour of the area churches. I love the Holy Land and all its reverent history, but how many pictures of rocky fields and locals dressed up as shepherds can you look at in one evening? Being there, near the footsteps of Jesus, is one thing. Watching color slides of the tour bus and Ezra, the Bethlehem guide, is another. Or, heaven forbid, it just might be the preacher, himself, with slides from his Montana vacation last summer. Snowcapped mountains, miles of Interstate 15 shot through the windshield of a 1987 Winnebago, and members of the Missoula Methodist church where he and his wife attended on Sunday morning.

"So that is why you don't go to 'hot dish suppers' anymore," you may say. Well, that's part of it. There's another reason, but I hesitate to share that one with you. But then I'm not here to tease, so why not? Okay, it's the food.

Tell me you've never known a neighbor or an aunt who had a cat who walked across the kitchen counters or slept in the pans under the sink. Need I say more?

You can know someone at church for years as a good and decent human being without knowing a thing about their personal hygiene. Does this make me a snob? I don't think so. Let's just say I'm playing it safe. I eat at home and send money to the missionaries and even though I might miss out on a little fellowship from time to time, I also might miss out on some food poisoning I heard about at another church recently. Ten people who were eating at the same table came down with the "flu" within two days of the dinner. Or maybe it was just too much macaroni and cheese and chocolate cake. Yeah, that's what it was. Sure.

THANK YOU FOR THE WORLD SO SWEET.
THANK YOU FOR THE FOOD WE EAT.
THANK YOU FOR THE BIRDS THAT SING.
THANK YOU GOD, FOR EVERYTHING.

Easter Best

*L*ike every six year old, I grew up faster in my mind than I did in anyone else's. I thought I was pretty hot stuff and thought I should look and dress and act like my older brother who was six years my senior. And one of the early contentions I can recall was the clash with my mother over what I should wear to church. Short pants in the summer was her choice and my sorrow. I cried and fought and yipped and threw as big a scene as

I had ever thrown over anything, and can still recall Daddy stepping in and settling the matter quickly and to everyone's satisfaction. Everyone's but mine. I wore the short pants and can honestly say I am no worse for the wear.

I do remember uttering something about "when I grow up I'll wear what I want to to church." A rather shallow and obvious statement, but what did I know at six years old? I also remember saying, "When I grow up I'll never eat liver." That one held true also, but has nothing to do with this particular story.

What people wear to church was once a serious matter to consider. All week long it was jeans and khakis and tennis shoes and t-shirts, and then come the Lord's Day, it was your Sunday best. Ours were often ill-fitted due to our constant growing, but they were always clean and pressed. We weren't wealthy, and quite frankly I never knew if we were poor or not but I do remember Mama always saying on the matter of clothes, "There's no disgrace in being poor, but there is also no excuse for being dirty." So we were clean and dressed for Sunday school and church. No jeans allowed. No sweatshirts. No ball jackets. It had to be a blue suit or a sport coat and always a tie. Good training by anybody's standard.

And this standard wasn't to show ourselves off, but was to show respect for where we were. I remember an old man who used to come in his bib overalls. That's all he had, so that was fine. Or a lady who wore the same dress every week. Again, nothing wrong with that. So what's the point, you may ask, to all this? Well, the point is not with those who don't because they can't, but with those who don't because they won't.

Go into any church of worship this Sunday morning and you'll see pre-teen kids and teenagers in jeans and ball jackets, not because that's all they have but because that's all the effort they're willing to make and all the instruction and guidance they're afforded by their parents. Who's to blame? You may feel no blame is in order and you may be right, but there's something innate down inside of me that cringes just a little when the denim hits the pew.

Grown men see nothing wrong with dressing down from what they wear to work everyday. They show up on Sunday looking like they might be going on a picnic. Short-sleeved shirts and open collars. When this shows up in the same family with the teenaged denim, then no explanation is necessary.

Then, of course, there's the *other* side. The overdressed and under-thought-out outfit that would look more compatible on a dance floor than in a sanctuary. And, look out now, it's usually a woman. And spring is usually the culprit that brings out the worst in fashion taste.

We all know that spring is the sign of re-birth. A new life for the plants and buds that make the world pretty. A doffing of Old Man Winter's heavy coat and a donning of light and airy breaths of beautiful colors and hues. And the resurrection of

Christ seems to key this inspiration in most churchgoers of any age and gender. You won't see much evidence at Easter sunrise service because it's still pretty nippy at 7 a.m. and most have to wear a coat. And they certainly don't want to cover up anything with last winter's coat. But cover your eyes for the morning worship. That's when the color splashes into the vestibule like drugstore cologne on the neck of a boy getting ready for his first date. Floral print dresses, matching hats, suits of every shade and style, and even the men show up in something just picked out and altered yesterday at the local department store. A new tie and new dress shirt that still has the horizontal creases across the front from being factory-folded.

Ah, we're a pretty bunch. And I, and you, too, have known people who just won't go to church on Easter morning unless they have a new outfit to wear. It's become a tradition. A habit. An obsession. A ridiculous ritual that belittles every reason for going to church, especially on Easter. But, ah, we're a pretty bunch. Or have I already said that?

Every minister in the world knows what C & E's are. Just ask them. They're the people who only come to church on Christmas and Easter. And more likely than not, they'll have a new outfit on each time. You know some.

We had a minister years ago, a wonderful old character whose friendship and memory I cherish, who was the most honest and straightforward human I've ever known. He never stood on ceremony and never bandied words. He spoke socially just as head-on as he preached the gospel. Eugene Jordan. I loved him and all he stood for. Whenever we sang "He Leadeth Me," I always liked getting to the last verse that goes:

AND WHEN MY TASK ON EARTH IS DONE,
WHEN BY THY GRACE THE VICTORY'S WON,
E'EN DEATH'S COLD WAVE I WILL NOT FLEE,
SINCE GOD THRO' JORDAN LEADETH ME.

I always felt there was some personal prophecy in that last line for our congregation.

Anyway, back to the C & E's and the Rev. Gene Jordan. I heard him stand up in the pulpit one Easter morning and face a packed church with extra chairs placed in the aisles to accommodate all the semi-annual members and say, "Good morning. Happy Easter and Merry Christmas. I say this because I won't see a lot of you again until December."

That was old-time religion at its best.

And the Christmas and Easter members and their fashion statements have had such an effect on me that to this day if I happen to buy a new suit or tie anywhere around the spring of the year, I make it a point *not* to wear it to church on Easter Sunday. My Easter best is something old. Just a little quirk of mine to show the proper respect to our Savior and to the Rev. Jordan.

HE LEADETH ME! HE LEADETH ME!
BY HIS OWN HAND HE LEADETH ME.
HIS FAITHFUL FOLLOWER I WILL BE,
FOR BY HIS HAND HE LEADETH ME!

Easter Sunrise Service

For as long as I can remember, we have always had one at our church. Getting up before daylight on the first Sunday after the first full moon following the spring equinox is a habit I just can't get out of.

As a kid, it was a novelty I looked forward to from year to year. Cold and still dark, I'd crawl out of bed and dress in my warmest Sunday clothes and we'd head for the front lawn of the church where everyone would stand for the 20 or 30-minute service. Somebody would sing. Somebody would pray. And somebody would tell the Resurrection story and then we'd all go back home to get warm and eat breakfast and come back again for the regular ten o'clock service. Somewhere in there, while we were home, we'd hunt the eggs.

I recall one year going to the "big" sunrise service. This was the citywide one where about a dozen churches went together and had one on a hill in the community cemetery. I was 11 years old, give or take a few months or years due to my memory, and had recently joined the Boy Scouts. In our uniforms, it was our job to direct traffic that year with our flashlights in our hands and frost coming out of our mouths. This only happened one year the best I remember and I really can't say if it was due to us not wanting to get that cold again or due to the three cars we directed into soft ground and which got stuck up to their hubcaps. Some things are best left unrecalled.

Then, as an adult, I always found that my sons looked forward to crawling out of bed in the early morning darkness as much as I did at their age. By this time, the clothes had changed though. Everyone was dressing for warmth and there was nary a tie to be seen in the foggy a.m. And I learned why Daddy seldom went with us years before. He stayed home for the same reason that I always made sure we took two cars; so I could make an excuse to leave a few minutes early and slip back home and hide the eggs. I miss doing that.

And all those years, not one in particular, but all of them together, taught me something about the Scriptures that you can't learn on one or two Sunday mornings. Of all of those years I stood in that dewy grass with cold feet and numb toes, and I still do, I never once heard a different message. It was always Mary Magdalene coming to the tomb with the other women and seeing the angel and running back and getting Peter. And then Peter and John racing toward the problem at hand and Peter peeking in when he got there and seeing the linens folded. Then Mary and the "gardener" talking and the "gardener" saying her name, "Mary," and then her joy at the recognition of whom she had been talking to and it all being capped with her exclamation to the disciples that she had seen the Lord!

Hearing that same story year after year and knowing that it would be told again and again was no reason to stay home. On the contrary, knowing I would hear it again and again is what kept me coming back. And I stand there every year with that Easter morning mist around me and the sun pulling itself up over the parking lot, and I want to tell every minister who has ever fretted over a new angle to keep the old, old story fresh, not to fret. Just tell it again. We all want to hear it. We all need to hear it. And on this morning, of all mornings, that's where we want to be. Where we need to be. A few quiet moments at the beginning of a long family day, in the garden with Mary and Jesus with our own thoughts and our own prayers. And then we, each one of us, can close our eyes and say as Mary did, "I have seen the Lord!"

Easter is the most peaceful day of the year.

I COME TO THE GARDEN ALONE,
WHILE THE DEW IS STILL ON THE ROSES:
AND THE VOICE I HEAR, FALLING ON MY EAR,
THE SON OF GOD DISCLOSES.
AND HE WALKS WITH ME AND HE TALKS WITH ME,
AND HE TELLS ME I AM HIS OWN;
AND THE JOY WE SHARE AS WE TARRY THERE,
NONE OTHER HAS EVER KNOWN.

Elmer Sensabaugh

My mother often carried crackers in her purse to feed me and keep me quiet during the morning worship service. This was, of course, before the advent of a nursery for pre-school children. Before the nursery, a lot of things passed as a pacifier during the morning service. I can remember seeing saltine crackers, Ritz crackers, ginger snap cookies, animal crackers, and car keys. Crackerjacks, popcorn, graham crackers, and leather billfolds. Anything a child could hold and chew was game.

Although, after the age of starting to school, nothing was game. You were on your own and for the sake of your physical well-being, you had better be on your best behavior. After the age of starting to school and before my teen years, the speech I most often got was, "You can sit through a double feature at the movies every Saturday morning so there is no reason you can't sit still for one hour in church." It's hard to argue with that kind of logic even at nine years old.

Every kid gets that speech in one form or another before they even get out of the car on Sunday mornings. "Once we sit down, there will be no going out and getting a drink of water in the middle of the sermon."

Or how about, "If you have to go to the bathroom, go now before we go into church, because once we're in there, we're in there to stay."

Or the parental favorite, "Don't make me have to take you out." This one was usually uttered in a low, slow voice with venom dripping on every word.

There were really only three rules my mother ever laid down to us with any regularity, but she was serious about these:

#1. Don't turn around and look at people behind you.

#2. Don't chew gum, but if you do, chew it with your mouth closed.

#3. Don't talk or squirm.

Now number one was never a big problem for me. I tried it a couple of times when I was still pre-school and to tell you the honest truth, it didn't take me long to learn that I just didn't bend that way. Now I have seen kids sit up on their knees and stare at the people in the pew behind them. I've even been one of those guys in the pew behind, and let me tell you it's an uncomfortable feeling. It's the same feeling as following a school bus through town. The kids on the back seat just stare out the window at you all through the stoplight. Then the same thing at the next stoplight. You finally make a turn and go out of your way just to get away from those relentless eyes. Except in a pew, there is no turn.

I've seen kids sit that way on their knees for 30 minutes. I never could. It's an unnatural position and I would rather have been sitting down on my behind, eating crackers.

Number two was always a mystery. I was never a big gum chewer and am still not. Until I see someone else chewing some. Then I have to have a stick right now. And that's pretty much the way I was as a kid. And my aunt, who was usually sitting on the other side of me, always had a coat pocket full of Juicy Fruit. And she was not scared of my mother, so she would give me a stick anytime I asked for it.

Now this thing about chewing with your mouth shut was something Mama had down pat. She was good at it. But I never learned the art. It's sock those jaws together and mash that juice out as hard and as quickly as possible. Sometimes it would pop.

Sometimes it would smack. And every time it would, Mama would look over the top of her glasses at me, and that was the most trouble you could be in. That glare and stern look with her head tilted and her eyes boring little beams of warning directly my way. That's when I'd drop my head and look the other way because I knew that the next time I made eye contact with her, she would be holding her hand out, palm up, demanding I spit the gum in it. Sometimes I did. Most times I did. A few times I swallowed it. And a few times I practiced chewing with my mouth shut like she had told me to in the first place. But it's no fun. It's like eating chicken with a fork. I'd just rather not do it at all.

And then there's number three. This one came the hardest and lasted the longest.

I guess I was about nine or ten, and I had a friend, Bobby, who was about the same age, and we would slide down the pew whenever there was room and sort of sit by ourselves. We'd talk till the service started and then we'd giggle a little during the hymns and then pass notes on the bulletin during the sermon. About the average type thing most nine and ten year olds do.

This one particular Sunday morning we had scooted just a little farther than usual and we wound up, by sermon time, at the far end of the pew from where my mother was sitting. Our antics must have gotten a little more animated than usual and even though I could feel her looking over the top of her glasses at me, I would not turn around and meet her eye. Being the lady she was, she was not inclined to scoot down the pew and grab me by the neck as some mothers might have done. She used her good sense and simply leaned forward and caught the eye of the man sitting in the pew directly behind me. She nodded to him her consent to stop the commotion that was going on in front of him, which he did with historical results.

His name was Mr. Elmer Sensabaugh, and as later years would prove to me, not a finer man ever darkened the doors of our Presbyterian sanctuary. He was a quiet man. A kind man. A gentle man. A man who never had kids of his own. Which was probably why he could afford to be so quiet, kind, and gentle. But of all his good and wonderful traits, there stands above that the one thing I remember most about him. He had the biggest hands and thickest fingers I'd ever seen. Or at least I thought at the time he had.

When Elmer got the nod, he didn't reach up and put his hand on my shoulder or on Bobby's. He didn't lean up and whisper in our ears to straighten up and quiet down. No, he took his middle finger and touched the fingernail to the inside of his big, ole, meaty thumb and flicked me on top of the head harder than Moe has ever hammered Larry. I froze and the waves from the thump shook the bench for two minutes. I saw angels and heard bells, but I never turned around or moved a muscle in my body until after the last hymn was sung.

It was unusual behavior on my part and on his. But it worked. We learn lessons from some of the most unlikely people and we remember some of the most unlikely things.

Elmer passed on many years ago, probably never remembering this incident and never having any inkling that I would remember it all these years and be sharing it with you now. We have to be careful of every small thing we do. Someone may be snapping a mental photo of the moment and we never know it.

As for me, I never talked again in church until I was 22 years old and I still can't grow hair on that spot on top of my head where Elmer Sensabaugh thumped me.

DO YOU HEAR THE BELLS NOW RINGING?
DON'T YOU HEAR THE ANGELS SINGING?
'TIS THE GLORY HALLELUJAH JUBILEE.
IN THAT FAR-OFF SWEET FOREVER,
JUST BEYOND THE SHINING RIVER
WHEN THEY RING THE GOLDEN BELLS
    FOR YOU AND ME.

The Family Pew

When you go into a movie theater, you have a certain place you like to sit. It may be on the back row or it may be near the front on the left or in the middle so that you're centered with the screen and you may even count rows before you sidle in and take your seat. But I'm betting it's something like this and not just a random seat in the dark. Everyone has a preference as to where they can see best or hear best or just feel most comfortable for no explanatory reason.

The same goes for church. Every family has a place they sit every Sunday morning and there had better not be any strangers or stragglers in the "family pew," or someone just might get glared at. There's something about what feels right. Something about owning the right to this particular section. Something about this is where my forefathers sat and where my children will sit and I don't want to be challenged or changed on the matter. It's my pew and I dare anyone to take it. The pewage, and yes, that's a word, in our church is 28. Fourteen on each side. Eight or 9 can sit comfortably in each one, and 10 or even 11 can squeeze in if a couple of them are kids or if someone is willing to sit forward. Quite frankly, I've never seen it so full that these numbers have been tested. There's always plenty of room and usually in the front. We Presbyterians tend to fill up from the back. That comes from a lot of possible reasons. We're too lazy to walk any farther down the aisle than we have to or we're shy and don't want to walk in front of any more people than we have to, or we might have to get up and go out during the service and we don't want to disturb any more people than we have to, and I could go on and on. Notice that each one had to do with not wanting to do any more than we have to. We own up to our shortcomings . . . when we have to.

The word "pew" comes from the French word *puie* and it means "a raised place." This, down through the ages, has come, somehow, to mean those benches we sit and sleep and squirm on once a week. And some of those benches are very ornate and pretty to the eye, yet hard to the touch. Some are slick and allow you to slide easily should some latecomer "move you over" to the center where no one wants to sit. Some are padded with rich-colored cushions that make your Sunday morning visits a little softer. Some are curved and fancy and some are plain and straight-backed and some are even short and cozy. But all of them have one thing for sure in common — they belong to someone.

I could walk you down the center aisle of our wonderful old place of worship on any given weekday and even though it would be empty, I could tell you the names of everyone, who was last Sunday and will be this Sunday, sitting in each pew. I could tell you the family names and who will sit on the ends and who will be sandwiched in the middle. I could tell you whose kids made the scuffmarks left on the backs of the pews and who scorched the cushion with dripping wax at a Christmas candlelight service. I could tell you who will arrive early before the church bells ring and who will arrive late after the first hymn has begun. I could tell you who left their bulletins laying in the seats and who left crumbs from animal crackers on the carpet. Family pews make for warm churches.

Facing the altar, the left side of the church is sometimes referred to as the Gospel Side. The right side is called the Epistle Side. That has always been ours, the Epistle Side. Six from the back. That's where you'll find us. That's the pew where my mother held me in her arms and fed me a bottle. That's the pew

I curled up and slept on during the sermon when I was 3 and 4 years old. That's the pew where I drew pictures on the bulletin inserts when I was 6 and 7. The pew I leafed through the Bible in and began memorizing the books of the Old and New Testament when I was 9 and 10. The pew I exited when I went up front to join the church when I was 12. The pew I walked past when I got married. The pew I sat in with my own family as my children came along.

That's the pew where my mother held the communion plates for me while I took the bread and drink and then passed them past me so I wouldn't risk dropping them. And that's the same pew where I do the same for her today.

Life goes on and I'll never sit anyplace else.

WILL THE CIRCLE BE UNBROKEN
BY AND BY, LORD, BY AND BY?
THERE'S A BETTER HOME A-WAITING
IN THE SKY, LORD, IN THE SKY.

Flowers, Coffee, and an Occasional Smoke

Some things are necessary to a church service, but some things are optional; some things are borderline and other things are outrageously out of place. Let's start with the optional.

Flowers. Now I don't know much about flowers, and to be completely honest with you, I never notice them. I don't see them if they're there and I don't miss them if they're not. But that's just me. I think it speaks to my gender.

But to most distaff, it is noticed, noted, and required. It becomes an integral and important part of the service to most women of the church. They plan the color scheme, pick the seasonal bouquets, and place them delicately in vases in the center or to each side of the pulpit, without fail, for every worship service. They enhance the atmosphere with nature's beauty and accelerate the air with perfumed aromas much like the incense the priests prepared in biblical days. And for those who feel it and need it, it's wonderful. For the few like me who appreciate it but don't know one plant from the other, it's a nice touch but I would probably put the money from the flower fund over into the fund to fix the leaky roof if I had my way.

I know about Easter lilies and Christmas poinsettias and not a whole lot more. I can recognize a rose and a tulip and I know now that phlox is something I should mow around and not down, even though I learned the hard way. I like the smell of lilacs and I know the religious legend that goes with the dogwood and I fell against a cactus one time in the desert. So I've had a little flower experience. I always buy my wife an orchid to wear on Easter Sunday and I've had to stick a boutonniere in my lapel for a few weddings from time to time. And on Mother's Day and Father's Day I've always loved that tradition of wearing a red carnation if your parent was alive and a white one if the respective parent was deceased. And let's see, that's about all I know about flowers.

Oh, I can spell and pronounce chrysanthemum and hyacinth and gladiolus and understand why people call them "glads," and I can recall with fondness the sweet smell of the honeysuckle that grew along the fencerow in left field when I played Little League. But I just don't know enough to be on the flower committee or help place the baby's breath and greenery around a Sunday morning floral arrangement. There've been fights in our congregation over what flowers should be up front.

Whenever someone has a Friday evening or Saturday afternoon wedding, they always leave token flowers in the sanctuary for Sunday morning. And that's a nice and grateful touch. But it also works the same for funerals. If there's a funeral during the week, the family will leave some leftovers on the table in front of the pulpit and one of the church ladies will come by on Saturday evening and decide that that particular spray looks too morbid or that particular frond is too big for the vase and they'll change it. Then the family of the recently laid-to-rest comes in on Sunday morning and sees some sweet Williams or African violets in their place, and all heliotrope breaks loose.

So leave me out of the optional part. Let me serve on the maintenance committee or the worship committee or even the finance committee. Leave the flowers to the ladies who know them and grow them. And God bless them, everyone.

Next come the borderline things in church and the ones that pop to mind the quickest are the refreshments.

I can remember when going to church was singing, praying, and preaching. When did coffee become as important as one of the sacraments? We never had coffee when I was a kid. It was years before we even had a water fountain and that was such a big deal I couldn't walk past it without getting a drink and splashing water all over the floor because the water pressure was too high and it would smack you in the face like a wet snowball every time you pressed the little button with the palm of your hand. Now some churches even have Coke machines!! And donuts! When did this all happen and why? To lure outsiders to join the church or to appease the already members who just couldn't get through another hour without a cup of caffeine? And it's not just a coffee room now where people stop before Sunday school and worship service, but every adult Sunday school room has their own pot with all the fixings, like sugar and substitute sugar and flavored creamers and plastic spoons and styrofoam cups.

And every adult Sunday school room has donuts, plain, glazed, and chocolate, and cupcakes and napkins. And you know what? It's pretty nice. Not necessary, but nice. Border-line. Can do without it, but wouldn't want to. Sometimes the coffee's a little stronger than I like and sometimes the donuts are a little more than "day old," but I can make it. Too many sweets sometimes. I might like a sandwich for a change and maybe a diet Pepsi, but I can make do. I can make it till lunch. If I have to.

And then there are those things that are so outrageously out of place but so much a part of our culture, it just wouldn't be church without them.

Go back in time with me. It's my childhood and yours. Mine was in the fifties and it gets more vivid with each passing year. The church bell rings and calls us all to worship and, for an hour, we do. And then the final hymn is sung and the preacher stands at the front door and shakes hands with everyone as they exit into the sunlight, and standing there on the front lawn of the church is a group of men, church leaders in their Sunday-best suits and dress hats, talking and . . . smoking. It's like coming out of a movie theater and seeing the men light up as they clear the door. Or watching them at a picnic and seeing them reaching in their shirt pockets for a pack of Camels as they finish their last bite of butterscotch pie. They're shaking hands with the preacher with one hand and shaking out a Lucky Strike with the other. It was as much a Sunday morning ritual as bowing your head when you prayed. As sure a sight as blue choir robes in the winter and white linen ones in the summer.

The women grouped together, the kids ran and played together, and the men stood and smoked together. The talk was varied. Sometimes it was the weather or hunting season or the economy, but the action was always the same. Daddies and uncles and all the men of the church, full of the Holy Spirit and R.J. Reynolds. Oh, I know it wasn't healthy. You don't have to

83

tell me that. Forget about that for a minute. It was the times. The easy, politically incorrect times. The innocent, summer-time memories of simple people on a church lawn after church, enjoying one another. Nobody stands around and talks any-more. That's why people drink coffee and smoke. When you're standing around or sitting around for a long time talking, you need something to do together. And smoking just happened to be it. I don't recommend re-creating the scene today, but I sure do miss the sight. Flowers, coffee, and an occasional smoke. They're all three pretty unnecessary to our salvation, but they're all a sincere part of our religious heritage, a sweet scene from our Christian childhood, and they all hold a special place in our hearts and in our Sunday morning memories.

I AM GOING TO A CITY
WHERE THE STREETS WITH GOLD ARE LAID,
WHERE THE TREE OF LIFE IS BLOOMING,
AND THE ROSES NEVER FADE.

HERE THEY BLOOM BUT FOR A SEASON;
SOON THEIR BEAUTY IS DECAYED.
I AM GOING TO A CITY
WHERE THE ROSES NEVER FADE.

Footwashing

The Thursday night before Easter, we all celebrate the sacrament of the Lord's Supper. We pass the bread and the drink, and in our own particular ways we partake of them both, and with bowed heads share in the spirit of the events that are about to take place over the next few days. This we, all Christians, have in common. This we, all Protestants, have in common.

But Martin Luther started a trend that has seen no end. Every denomination breaking off and going in their own selected direction, doing things in their own selected way. Matthew, Mark, and Luke didn't know anything about the washing of the feet. John is the only one who told us about that. He said as the evening meal was being served, Jesus got up from the table, wrapped a towel around his waist and poured water into a basin, and proceeded to wash the feet of his disciples. Simon Peter immediately rebelled and said, "You shall never wash my feet."

This is, of course, a beautiful and spiritual story and one that teaches us to serve one another as Jesus has served us. And the meaning and the truth is not lost on any of us, but let me take the liberty to say that if the Catholics can consider Peter to be the first Pope because of the statement, "Upon this rock I will build my church," then we can consider Peter to be the first Presbyterian in not wanting his feet washed.

I have never been to a foot-washing ceremony, but it must be a very humbling experience. I would like to go and maybe even participate just to know the feeling. Just to feel what Peter and the other disciples felt. I think it could be as moving as the sacrament of the Last Supper and on a human realm, maybe even more so. Maybe next year I'll go to a Mennonite church or a Primitive Baptist church and see for myself what takes place. I understand the women wash the women's feet and the men the men's. They even tie the sash around their waist exactly as Jesus did. They're washed all with the same water and dried with the same towel. Brothers and sisters in the spirit and in the body.

I'll do this, but I don't think I'll be bringing it back to my church. I think it would be met with some opposition. It would be like asking the Episcopalians to sing Southern Spirituals. Like asking the Seventh Day Adventists to go to church on Sunday. Like suggesting a Methodist go to confession. Or suggesting a Christian Scientist go to a doctor. Until someone finds records of John Calvin and John Knox washing one another's feet, I don't think it's even a possibility.

> JESUS PAID IT ALL;
> ALL TO HIM I OWE;
> SIN HAD LEFT A CRIMSON STAIN;
> HE WASHED IT WHITE AS SNOW.

Funerals

I like it when the church is used for varied and sundry things. As you've probably noted, we've used ours for Boy Scout meetings and softball games and Halloween and birthday parties and just about anything else you can think of. We've even shown movies in the fellowship hall and at one time had a room for ping pong and shuffleboard. If the church is the center, what goes on around it can't be all that bad.

And one of the main functions for any church building worth its weight in mortar and stone is the funeral. It's an unpleasant yet comforting necessity. It seems, however, more and more today, that the church is not used as much for funerals as it has been in the past. The funeral home is popular and I think I know the reason for that. It's hard walking back into a house of worship on Sunday morning after just laying a loved one to rest that same week. The acrid smell of the flowers is still hanging thickly in the air and the image of sadness permeates from every corner of the sanctuary. And it's not just that Sunday morning after. The memory is never quite gone even years later. Some may find this comforting, but I think many find it disturbing.

I can remember being at my grandmother's funeral at another church in another town years ago. She had passed away suddenly one weekday afternoon and as I sat there listening to her preacher eulogize her, my eyes wandered around the walls and the pews and the stained glass windows, and I thought that only a few days ago, just last Sunday, she was sitting here in one of these seats, singing from one of these hymnals, listening to this same minister, never realizing that would be her last knowing visit. And there we were, just days later, getting ready to carry her out of those old familiar doors she had walked out of so many times on her own.

I was glad I wouldn't have to go back there every Sunday and be reminded. I was glad that wasn't my church. I suddenly, and for all time, understood the purpose of the funeral home chapel.

When I look down that center aisle in my mind's eye, in retrospect, in my memory, I want to see a pretty spring bride in a long white gown, smiling up at her new fresh-faced husband. I want to see three little seven year olds in bathrobes and fake beards carrying tissue boxes spray-painted gold. I want to see the choir marching in and the deacons and the elders taking up collection. What I don't want to see is a steel gray casket, draped in flowers, being wheeled out in front of a grieving family.

Of all the things we do at church, this is the one service I could gladly sacrifice to another locale. Arriving in heaven is a happy and glorious occasion for the honored guest, but it's a sad departure for those left behind. And aren't they the ones this ceremony is really for? The dearly departed has no need for such earthly sentiments. Heaven is waiting and the doors are open. Family and friends are watching on the other side. A lifetime of prayers has been answered. The church is for those left behind. Those gone on are no longer in need.

SWEET HOUR OF PRAYER,
SWEET HOUR OF PRAYER,
MAY I THY CONSOLATION SHARE?
TILL FROM MOUNT PISGAH'S LOFTY HEIGHT,
I VIEW MY HOME AND TAKE MY FLIGHT:
THIS ROBE OF FLESH I'LL DROP AND RISE,
TO SEIZE THE EVERLASTING PRIZE;
AND SHOUT WHILE PASSING THROUGH THE AIR,
FAREWELL, FAREWELL, SWEET HOUR OF PRAYER.

Glossolalia

Considering my whitewashed, well-protected, Presbyterian upbringing, I'm surprised I even know this word. Where did it come from? Is it in the Bible? Well, no it isn't. But what it means is in the Bible. It means "speaking in tongues" and there is plenty of that in the Bible. None in the Presbyterian Church, mind you, but then there are any number of things between the covers of the Holy Book that you won't find in the halls or homes of a good Presbyterian.

Baptizing in the river? Washing of the feet? One-cup communion? Thank you just the same, but I think we've covered all of that. Then how about a "Praise the Lord" or an occasional "Amen" if you hear something that moves you during the service? Would you consider that? No, ma'am, we would not. We don't yell out anything here. We're Presbyterian and we may wake someone.

The only "amens" you'll ever hear between our stained glass windows are at the end of a prayer and the end of a song. If we like something the preacher said and was especially moved by his sermon, we just wait and tell him about it as we're going out the door and shaking hands with him. It's quieter this way.

The first time I heard an "amen" was in a church I was visiting and it was also the first glossolalia I experienced. It's something you don't forget easily, especially if you're a teenager of 16. We had been invited to sing, my brother and two friends and myself, at a small country church. It was a Sunday night service and the denomination eludes me after all these years, but it must have been Pentecostal. The place was packed and the heat was high and we sang a few songs and, considering their applause, they liked it sufficiently enough.

After a short musical program from us, they began their service with us stuck on the front row, so we stayed and worshiped with them. It was during the announcements that the speaker was making about some upcoming events that I heard my first "amen." It startled me for just a second. The next one sort of hit me as funny (remember I was 16). And, by the third one, I was getting accustomed to the ambiance. The four of us looked at each other and then around the little church as best we could and decided among ourselves, that even though we were among strange customs, we were among good people.

I held this thought in reverence until the next revelation of the night hit my young ears. When the speaker asked for everyone to rise for a word of prayer, I got much more than I ever expected. The congregation rose and began to pray out loud. All in different tongues and all at the same time. It must have been what the original Day of Pentecost sounded like.

Now we Presbyters know that as far back as Isaiah there is mention of "strange tongues." And we know that Paul, himself, placed his hands on converts and they began to speak in tongues. But we also know that Paul was not all that hot on it. He said he could and did speak in tongues but that he would rather speak five words someone could understand than ten thousand words they couldn't understand. He said, "What good is it if no one knows what you're saying?" He even went so far as to say if you don't have an interpreter, you might as well keep your mouth shut.

So here I stood, with Paul on my side, not knowing which way to look or run. Seventy-five people all talking a different tongue and at the top of their voice. But that, even, was not as unnerving as the preaching I was about to witness in the pulpit for the next 45 minutes. This man shouted and paced and yelled and strutted and climbed up on the little railing in front of the choir and bounced up and down and jumped off and ran and screamed till he was red in the face. He pounded and waved his fists and clenched his jaw and cried and finally broke into a tongue of his own that sounded like Apache talk from a Rory Calhoun western. This only tended to inflame the congregation more. They yelled their "Amens" and "Praise the Lords" and stomped and cried right along with him.

When he was through, he was wet from head to toe. He had sweated through his suit coat, his hair was in his crimson face, and he was panting like an overweight marathon runner. This is when the original speaker came back up front to give the benediction and said, "We want to thank brother Haines for that fine message. For all you visitors with us tonight, we're sorry our minister could not be here. Brother Haines is a lineman for the telephone company and was good enough to fill in at the last minute."

This was my introduction to "tongues of fire." I came, I heard, and I left just as fast as I could. It's not for everyone, but it's an education.

Thank you, Paul.

O FOR A THOUSAND TOUGUES TO SING
MY DEAR REDEEMER'S PRAISE,
THE GLORIES OF MY GOD AND KING,
THE TRIUMPHS OF HIS GRACE.

Halloween

I understand they can't have Halloween parties in school anymore. Too naughty and evil and demonic. The parties, not the schools.

Well, we always took care of that problem. We covered the demons and the goblins by having our Halloween parties at church. Strange place for such a party, you say? Not at all. What better place to gather a bunch of kids on Halloween night, that you wanted to keep out of trouble and out of danger, than the basement of the neighborhood church?

And it wasn't just for the kids. There were costume contests for all age groups. Young and old alike would dress up as witches and clowns, hoboes and devils, and the old women would dress up as old men and the old men would dress like old women, and everyone would take pictures and laugh and eat. And you know, if you can laugh and eat, there's not a much better time you can have.

The little kids would bob for apples. I remember one year there was a tent set up and an old fortune-telling gypsy (one of the Sunday school teachers) would tell scary futures to all who entered and lent her their hand.

Most years the teen classes would decorate the walls and mark off a couple of Sunday school rooms and lay out a "Chamber of Horrors" that you would have to walk through in the dark. Cobwebs would hit you in the face and shadows would jump at you and you would come across platters of peeled grapes that a voice from nowhere would tell you were eyeballs. Loud, haunted house laughter would run the girls into the darkened hallway where a hand would grab their feet from under a table, and there would be more screams and shrieks.

And then there was cider and gingersnap cookies and the unmasking of some of the better costumes and then everyone would go home and wait for Thanksgiving.

Many people think this is taking church social life much too far. We never did. It wasn't wicked and evil. It was cartoon evil. Cartoon wickedness. And for those who think Halloween should be banned as a bad influence, let me ask you if you really believe in Bugs Bunny. When Elmer Fudd takes a shotgun after old Bugs or the Wile E. Coyote gets hit over the head with another anvil, I don't stand up in the theater and yell "Murder!" It's a cartoon. And that's what Halloween is to a kid. Cartoon mischievousness. Lighten up.

One year our minister dressed as a woman. A very ugly woman, I might add. He wore a hat and veil and high heels and a print dress and pearls and white gloves and stockings. And he went unrecognized until the last minute when he was unmasked and given the prize for the best costume. No one knew who he was but me. I recognized the dress. His wife had worn it to church just two weeks before.

BRIGHTEN THE CORNER WHERE YOU ARE!
BRIGHTEN THE CORNER WHERE YOU ARE!
SOMEONE FAR FROM HARBOR
YOU MAY GUIDE ACROSS THE BAR;
BRIGHTEN THE CORNER WHERE YOU ARE!

Hymnbooks

I grew up in the Presbyterian church. Well, I don't mean I lived there. I didn't actually eat and sleep there in the pews. Yet, on second thought, I have slept in a few Presbyterian pews in my life. And to be even more honest, I have eaten there, too. I've already told you about the crackers my mother carried to feed me during the sermon back before we had a nursery for the younger non-members of the congregation. So I suppose it would be accurate to say that, yes, I grew up in the Presbyterian church.

Olivet Presbyterian Church it was. And still is. It's still there and so am I. Every Sunday morning it and I reacquaint ourselves with one another. The same pews. The same stained glass windows decorated with Bible verses and Good Shepherd paintings. The same pulpit that houses the preacher and hides the sound system. The same choir that grows a little older each year as I do and only changes when a new member can be talked into or tricked into or coerced into adding to its number. The same little communion glass holders on the back of the seats. The same collection plates. But not the same hymnbooks.

The hymnbooks are a point of contention with me. Through my years there, I've seen many hymnbooks come and go. Redback ones. Blueback ones. Greenback ones. Even paperback ones. And just when you seem to get comfortable with one, the women of the church or the youth group or the some-such-or-other Bible class decides its time to raise money for new hymnals. Just let the backs get a little worn on one of them or let some restless kid (who should be in the nursery eating crackers) mark inside one with a pencil, and somebody is up and running toward a bookbinder screaming for a new, updated hymnbook with new, updated hymns. And therein lies the problem.

I hate new hymns almost as bad as I hate new recipes. If there's nothing wrong with the old ones, let them and me be.

I like old hymnbooks because each one is full of memories. Every scar and rip was put there by somebody's child who is holding it down for his or her child to sing from now. Every broken spine and worn corner and stained cover has its story. The spine was broken when it was dropped by a visiting family who came in during the first hymn one morning and Elwood Balsley came down out of the choir and handed them a book already turned to the correct page because they looked lost and confused. The corners were worn from sliding them into the cradles on the back of each seat after each song for years of Sundays. And the big stain on the one in the fifth pew from the back on the right-hand side came from someone bumping their Mama's arm during communion when they were passing the tray with those little, tiny glasses of grape juice. Eight of those little tiny glasses can make a pretty big stain. And a pretty big noise, but that's another story.

A hymnbook is a hit and deserves to live to a good old age, just as Abraham did, when it finds a place in your heart so deeply entrenched that you have memorized all your favorite page numbers. I remember back in my pre-teen years, we used to have what we called a "song service" every Sunday night. It was always at 7:30 and only in the summertime as I remember it. I have often wondered why it was only in the summer and my only reasoning is so it wouldn't interfere with television shows. Back then, reruns started in May and ran through August and I can remember my daddy going to those song services and I know for a fact that he would not have gone in the winter and missed "Maverick." So it had to be summer.

We would do nothing but sing. After each song, someone would yell out his or her favorite song, not by title, but by page number. "Number 43," someone would say and the preacher, Mr. Parker, would turn to page 43 and say the title while the organ played the first verse and then we'd all sing. And after that one was over, the same thing would happen. A page number would be shouted from another corner of the church and the preacher would take charge and the organist would play and we would all sing. Seldom was there a lull. But sometimes, of course, there was. Sometimes when one song ended, the minister would have to coax someone to come up with a page number. And he'd wait and look all around the church and you'd hear people coughing and squirming and he'd just keep on waiting like the silence never embarrassed him or made him uneasy. But it did me. And that's when I first yelled out a number. I must have been ten years old, and just to ease the tension from all that silence and staring, I called out, "Page 97."

And from then on, there was hardly a week went by that I didn't yell out a page number. And more likely than not, it was page 97. Oh, I liked 129 and 64 and could actually sing the tenor part on 106. I sang the aftertime and what I thought was bass on 75 and 22. I was tempted a few times to call out one between 79 and 93 because they were all Christmas carols. Of course, I didn't. I was scared to, but I sure thought it would be funny if someone did.

And that is what I miss most every time someone wants to supply the pews with a new hymnbook. I miss the familiarity. The comfortableness. The touch and the sight of the old covers and the print that has grown so friendly to the eye. I miss those songs not being where they're supposed to be. I miss them not being in the order they should be in. I miss the titles not being by the numbers they should be by. I don't want some new hymn that I've never heard of and can't follow the melody to being 129. I don't want something that sounds like a chant to be on page 106. I don't want new words to old tunes and omitted verses that brought me comfort to get lost and never find their way into a more updated, theologically proper hymnal. I want 64 and 75 and 22. I want to call out "Number 97," and when I do I want the whole congregation to stand up and sing:

AT THE CROSS, AT THE CROSS,
WHERE I FIRST SAW THE LIGHT,
AND THE BURDEN OF MY HEART ROLLED AWAY.
IT WAS THERE BY FAITH,
I RECEIVED MY SIGHT,
AND NOW I AM HAPPY ALL THE DAY.

Laying on of Hands

The laying on of hands is a very personal thing. You have to actually touch that other person. You have to come in personal contact. You have to get close and show warmth and concern and emotion and passion to that other human being. And this is just not the Presbyterian way.

I have seen the laying on of hands in many other churches. I've certainly seen it on television. On TV it's used for healing. I watched Oral Roberts touch people back in the fifties in black and white and saw cripples throw away their crutches and the prone get up and walk and the blind see and the deaf hear, just like in the New Testament. Being an ever-suspicious coldwater Presbyterian, I never knew for sure if I was watching a church service or a carnival show. Oh, I believed it could happen. I believed God healed. But even as a kid I felt that God acted and healed on His own schedule and not on a television schedule full of commercials and station breaks and timed to go off exactly on the hour. (It always amazed me as a kid how those wrestling matches always ended just before that last beer ad. Never, not even once, was a match still in progress as the credits rolled.)

And I noticed the same thing with the TV preachers. The big healings came toward the end of the show in a fast and dramatic frenzy. And they just didn't lay on the hands, they sometimes socked 'em pretty good. Benny Hinn is still doing it today. He smacks people in the head and they fall back, risking greater physical injuries than they came to have cured. And it's all done in the name of God. And if this is all right with God, then it's certainly all right with me. It's just that I've always found God to work His mysterious ways in His own time frame.

We don't do a lot of physical healing in our little church. I don't think I can ever remember anyone being wheeled down the aisle on a Sunday morning and the preacher beating him up and sending him out the door running. What we do is we pray.

We pray for God to heal them in the way He best sees fit. And we have had some miracles. We have had people back in the pews who only days before were in the hospital on death's bed. We've had diseases eased and cured that medical science had given up on. And we have seen families and friendships mended and healed that were thought to have been hopelessly broken and divided.

We don't anoint with oil but I don't doubt its effect. We don't profess that the wine actually turns into the blood of Jesus, but I don't doubt its possibility. And we don't handle snakes even though Jesus told us we should have the faith to do so. We have never moved a mountain but I believe that faith can do that also, just like the New Testament tells me it can.

And while I'm being brazenly honest, I'll recant on something I may have misled you a little bit on. We *do* lay on the hands in one of our rituals. It's not for healing or anointing but for ordaining new elders. Whenever a new elder is elected, he comes up front and all the old elders gather round him and place their hands on his head and ordain him into the fold. This is the closest thing we get to emotion. A Baptist friend, knowing our somewhat stiff ways, once asked me if all the elders wore rubber gloves on those Sundays.

His cynicism and humor did not go unnoticed and his suggestion did not go unappreciated. I may bring it up at the next session meeting.

PRECIOUS LORD, TAKE MY HAND,
LEAD ME ON, HELP ME STAND.
I AM TIRED, I AM WEAK, I AM WORN.
THRU THE STORM, THRU THE NIGHT,
LEAD ME ON TO THE LIGHT.
TAKE MY HAND, PRECIOUS LORD,
LEAD ME HOME.

Miss Ora Hopkins

I have always had an extra dose of imagination. As a kid, my thoughts could run wild on any subject and at any time. And church seemed to offer just all kinds of opportunities for the mind to drift and create and explore things that should be left alone.

The first opportunity every Sunday morning was during the morning prayer. Now I learned to pray at a very early age and I knew you were supposed to thank God for all His blessings and then ask for more blessings and then ask for forgiveness and then pray for the people you liked and then say "Amen." That pretty much covered it for a boy my age and I managed to do pretty well on my own every night before I went to bed and everyday at school when I got into trouble and every time I told a lie and every time I. . . . Well, I think you see the pattern. I pretty much used prayer the way most people do. When I needed it.

And that morning prayer just didn't hold my attention the way it should. Our minister prayed long and hard and sincerely, but the more he went on, the more my mind would drift away. I'd pull it back, but then it would drift off again and I'd snap it back and try a little harder and then let go and the next thing I'd know I'd be herding cattle somewhere in the old West and saving pretty girls from bad guys and the organ playing the refrain and the choir singing, "A-MEN, A-MEN, AH-AH-AH-AH- MEN," would jar me back to reality and the present.

The next opportunity would come during the morning sermon. Now I have learned in my adult years that a sermon lasts approximately 20 minutes. But then I would have sworn it was the whole hour. I would tell myself that this morning was going to be different. This time I was going to listen to every word he said and follow every story he told and be just as attentive as those people in the choir looked like they were being. And every time I'd last about 45 seconds and then I'd be off again on some adventure. Off on something that happened to me last week at school or was going to happen to me next week at school, but more than likely off on something that would never happen to me ever, at all, in my lifetime.

Saving beautiful girls from dangerous, evil men was a favorite. Riding in a hero's parade was pretty big. Winning the World Series in the bottom of the ninth was very high on the charts. And when my creative juices ran a little dry, coloring in the a's, b's, d's, e's, g's, o's, p's, and q's in the bulletin with a pencil proved to be quite a time filler.

But the one scenario that always haunted my idle and empty head on these sacred Sunday mornings was the fantasy of rescue. For some reason I always had a fear of someone bursting through the front doors of the sanctuary with a gun and robbing everyone in the pews and then going down the center aisle and emptying the collection plates and passing through the choir loft and taking money and watches and rings. This, of course, is where my heroics would kick in and I'd somehow trip the culprit or disarm him or clip him a good one on the jaw the way Wild Bill Elliott did, and someone would grab his pistol and the police would be called and all would be saved.

What you must remember is that this was long before you heard things like this actually happening on the evening news. I have read actual news stories in recent years that were not far from the ones I dreamed up there in the wooden pews of my childhood. And why not? When are we more vulnerable than when we're in church? No one is armed. We all have money in our pockets and money in the plates and we are all supposed to be good Christians who just might turn the other cheek rather than put up a fight the way I had in my imagination. It's a scary scene that only a kid or a criminal could think up. But there you go. It was one of my favorites.

But no matter in what direction my creative thinking took me, the theme was always the same. Rescue. Saving someone. Helping a helpless situation. And believe it or not, I saw it played out in reality right before my eyes when I was about nine years old. No guns involved. No robbers. No bad guys of any kind.

Just a scene of rescue and help in the middle of a morning sermon, and it is as indelible on my mind today as it was that spring Sunday morning with the windows open and the breeze blowing through and the smell of something blooming on the trees in the churchyard. Someone else was the hero, of course, but I soaked it all in, wide-eyed and astounded.

There was a little old lady, who was both very old and very little, and her name was Miss Ora Hopkins. And everyone called her Miss Ora regardless of their age. She had money and no particular family that I knew of. She was driven to church every Sunday morning by someone, a nephew, a neighbor, a chauffer, I didn't know exactly who, but he would drop her off and she would walk down the aisle and sit in the second pew from the front. Miss Ora, who never married, was rumored to be in her early nineties and she dressed the part. High lace collars, hats, long skirts. All these things were important characteristics in my mind along with the fact of how little she was. Tiny. I'm guessing five-feet and 90 pounds. So small that when we stood to sing, I couldn't tell if she did or not. She was the same size sitting as standing from where I sat, which was about four rows back from her. One Sunday morning in May, just after we had sung the second hymn and Mr. Parker had read the morning Scripture, and he was well into his sermon of the day, as fate would have it, I was actually paying attention and my eyes were straight ahead just where they should have been. A slow and out-of-the-ordinary movement pulled my attention and my vision away from the pulpit. Miss Ora was falling over in her seat. Very slowly, as if pushed over by a warm wind blowing in the opened stained-glass window, she just tilted to her left and disappeared in the pew.

I startled and looked over at Mom who sat up on the edge of the seat. Mr. Parker stopped abruptly and seemed to gesture toward Miss Ora. I don't know if he was pointing or just instinctively reaching out, even though he was 15 feet away from her. But a murmur came over the congregation and people began to move toward her. The hero-of-the-moment was a deacon, John Varner, who was sitting across the aisle or maybe standing in the vestibule after taking up the collection. I'm not real sure, because I never saw exactly where he came from. All I know is that all of a sudden he was there, running to her pew, picking her up as if she were a babe in arms, and carrying her down the aisle and out the front door.

Church service stopped for only a few moments. The rescue squad was called and Miss Ora was taken to the ER and released and sent home in time for Sunday dinner.

The next Sunday, she was there on the second pew from the front just like always, and John Varner was there taking up collection just like always. And life was good. But I never looked at either one of them the same after that. She, small and frail, five-foot and 90 pounds, yet strong enough at 90-some years to bounce back and be there the next week just as if nothing at all ever happened. And he, strong, robust, 30 years old, the hero who carried her out like a bird in his arms, and saved her life and all right there in the middle of a sermon.

Some things in reality, no matter how large or small, are just downright better than anything, even I, could have ever dreamed up in my idle and empty mind.

EACH DAY I'LL DO A GOLDEN DEED
BY HELPING THOSE WHO ARE IN NEED;
MY LIFE ON EARTH IS BUT A SPAN,
AND SO I'LL DO THE BEST I CAN.

Money

I always had a nickel or a dime to put in the collection plate when I was growing up. It didn't add much to the building fund or the current expenses, but it created a habit in me that has lasted a lifetime. I feel guilty if a collection passes me and I don't add something to it. In my home church I always have an envelope to place in the plate. If I'm visiting a church somewhere else in the world, I always make sure I have extra money in my pocket for the offering just like I make sure I have extra money for popcorn when I go to the movies. I'd feel like a freeloader if I didn't add my "two-cents worth."

I have a friend, Bobby, who is an elder in our church today, who tells a wonderful story I'd love to claim as mine own, but I won't do that to him. He was eight years old or so and he and his family would walk the two blocks to church. He always passed a little store that was open on Sunday because the owners were Seventh Day Adventists. He would sneak in the store with some lame excuse each Sunday morning and buy a candy bar with the dime his mother always gave him for Sunday school. Then before Sunday school started, he and another eight-year-old friend, Skipper, would go out behind the church, break the candy bar in half and he'd sell half of it to Skipper for a dime. Skipper could afford the inflated price and never questioned it, as there was no place else to get half a Hershey bar at 10 a.m. on a Sunday morning. (Sort of like that popcorn in the movies I was talking about. You'll pay any price they want cause it's the only game in town at the time.) A lesson in basic economics will show you that this was a good deal for Bobby. He got his dime back and still got to eat half a Hershey.

And this was all well and good for as long as it lasted. Except the inevitable finally happened. One Sunday morning, Skipper didn't show up for church. Family vacation, summer camp, the flu. Whatever the reason, no Skipper, and Bobby is stuck with a candy bar and no money to put in the Sunday school plate. He panicked because he was sure his teacher would rat on him to his mother that he didn't put any money in the little basket when it was passed around.

He lived in fear all that morning and all that day and all that week, just waiting for something to be said. Fortunately for him, nothing was noticed and nothing ever happened, but he learned a lesson about gambling at an early age that has stuck with him until this very day.

Money has always been a big part of the church. Until you serve on a board of deacons or a session or a council of some sort, you never realize just how much business goes on in a church. You never realize how much it takes to just pay the bills. Sometimes the business of it all gets in the way of the spiritual and you have to step back and maybe even step down for a year or so to get your perspectives in the right places again.

Jesus knew how hard it was for money and church to mix and keep an honest tone to it. He went in and turned over the tables of the moneychangers to show his anger and concern. But at the same time there were rich women who traveled with Him and His disciples who gave money to their cause just to keep them going. His band of apostles even had a treasurer who carried the moneybag. Of course, that treasurer was named Judas and money turned out to be the least of his problems.

My daddy had a favorite old hymn he used to sing to himself while he was driving or working in the garden or just sitting in the back yard on a summer night. The song had a financial theme along with the religious message and it comes to mind now with some words of advice he gave me in his last years concerning the church and money. He told me, "Son, always remember the more you give, the more you'll receive."

He went on to explain that that should never be the reason for the giving, but that it would be the result of the giving. He was a wise man. That was over 35 years ago and I still miss him today as if I just saw him last night. And sometimes I do see him, sitting in the back yard on a summer night.

LONG AGO (DOWN ON MY KNEES),
LONG AGO (I SETTLED IT ALL),
YES, THE OLD ACCOUNT WAS SETTLED
    LONG AGO.
AND THE RECORD'S CLEAR TODAY,
FOR HE WASHED MY SIN AWAY,
WHEN THE OLD ACCOUNT WAS SETTLED
    LONG AGO.

Revival

This word conjures up a lot of things in most people's minds. Wild, nightly, shouting-at-the-top-of-your-voice, fervent preaching and the singing of old-timey hymns with folks running up and down the aisles with their hands in the air. Baptizing in the spirit, speaking in tongues, and just a general holy chaos.

And they wouldn't necessarily be wrong. But need I tell you it wasn't like this in the Presbyterian way? We used to have revivals with no shouting, running, or hollering. If a Presbyterian is seen doing any of these three things, it usually means something is on fire. And it ain't necessarily their soul. It's more than likely their house, their car, or the seat of their pants.

We Calvinists tend to take our religion and our revivals the way we take our oatmeal. Lukewarm with a little sugar, a little milk, and not too often. We've had a few revivals through the years, but the one I remember most was when I was six years old. Two brothers from Greensboro, North Carolina, Phil and Ben Saint, came and held services every night for a two-week period in the fall. How do I remember this when I was only six years old? When you encounter a preacher named Rev. Saint, you don't forget him easily.

Brother Ben was the musician. He sang solos, directed the choir, and led the congregation in old familiar spirituals. I remember he was tall. Not Daddy tall, but basketball tall. He stood heads above the other adults and sang louder than anyone in the choir and threw his arms and impressed the faithful and cynical alike. I watched him closely. He scared me a little bit. But then I've never had respect for anything or anybody that didn't scare me a little bit.

The Rev. Phil Saint was the evangelist half of the team. He preached. But he didn't stop there. He had an additional talent that set him apart and drew quite a crowd from the surrounding communities. While he preached his nightly sermon, he painted a picture on a canvas that was sitting on an easel behind the pulpit. He painted a picture pertaining to the message he delivered and at the end of the sermon there was a complete religious painting in full and vibrant color for all the world to see. What a gimmick! What a talent! What a revival!

These guys were good. Not your hot-blooded, getting-a-load-up-to-go-tonight kind of preachers. Not your red-in-the-face, fire-in-the-belly, day-of-Pentecost reformers. But artists. One who sang and one who painted. And the effect was lasting and sincere. And maybe it was because they were sincere.

On the last evening of their fortnight engagement, we held the first service ever in our spanking new educational building. At the end, a final offering was taken for the Saint brothers, as it had been each night, but this time it had a different twist. Rev. Phil got up and handed the plate back to our minister and said this was their donation to our building fund. Years later, I learned it was in the amount of $180.25. Not a large fortune, but in 1951 it was probably a pretty good night's work for the two of them and it certainly made a meaningful dent in our struggling budget.

Good deeds sometimes go unrewarded but seldom are forgotten. To this very day, hanging in that educational building, is a painting of Phil Saint's, signed and framed and on a wall that he helped build.

Revival is good and so were the Saints.

REVIVE US AGAIN, FILL EACH HEART
    WITH THY LOVE;
MAY EACH SOUL BE REKINDLED WITH
    FIRE FROM ABOVE.

HALLELUJAH! THINE THE GLORY.
HALLELUJAH! AMEN.
HALLELUJAH! THINE THE GLORY.
REVIVE US AGAIN.

Rock and Roll Heaven

In just about any church you go into today of any size, you will find an elaborate state-of-the-art sound system. Giant speakers; woofers and tweeters. You may even find a "sound room" somewhere behind the pulpit area that looks like engineer heaven. Amplifiers and knobs and pots and cords for input and output. Red lights blinking and green lights on standby and coils of cable and boxes of microphones. Church has become a show.

I've been in churches that have "the" sound system and whenever someone in the choir sings a solo, they reach over and take a mike off a stand and belt their stanza into it like they were on MTV. And I've been in churches that no longer show faith in their organists when it comes to those special solos. They have a friend, a husband, a boyfriend, an assistant, or something comparable, back in the "sound room" standing ready with a tape in hand. When the right moment comes, the assistant pops the tape in and an 80-piece orchestra begins the strands of some non-musical, new age religious song that no one can recognize and no one will be humming as they drive home.

And after this invisible orchestra plays an introduction the length of most cantatas, the singer puts his or her lips way too close to the metal netting on the microphone, and shrill and strident feedback bounces off the stained glass windows on the back wall and a squeal that would wake the dead from 40 funerals fills the sanctuary and creates a moment in religious history that will still be cringed at when the singer *and* the song are long forgotten. Do I long for an unplugged choir singing "Church in the Wildwood," accompanied by a slightly out-of-tune upright piano? You bet I do.

And then there's the preacher. Now I don't like a red-faced preacher who constantly yells at his parishioners and pounds his fist on the top of his pulpit. And neither do I like a preacher who mumbles in his shirt collar and stares mostly at his notes or the floor and speaks in conversational tones to where only the first and second row have a chance of deciphering his message. I ought to have a chance at it in the back, too. So that's when the Worship Committee meets and decides it's time to buy a sound system for the hard-of-hearing, the elderly, and the late-comers on the back row.

The first system was a simple creature. One little box with an off and on switch; one knob for tone and one for volume. Set that on a shelf at about knee level under the pulpit, plug a mike cord in it and mount the microphone on the top of the pulpit and center it with that little ribbon that runs down the middle of the preacher's Bible as a bookmark, run some cords down the side aisles under the carpet and put a speaker in a windowsill on each side of the congregation, and you're in show business. And that was good for a lot of years.

Oh, there were Sunday mornings when the deacons forgot to turn it on when they opened up the church and got things ready for worship. And there were Sunday mornings when it squealed a little or when someone complained it was too loud or too low and one of the ushers would have to sneak up behind the preacher and adjust the volume in hopes no one saw him. And, of course, everyone saw him and lost total track of what was being said and some kids snickered and the preacher jumped and the usher jumped and then the adults snickered and then guffawed and then the entire service came to a stop because we had a sound system, not because we didn't have a sound system.

But these problems were not enough. The preachers then decided they were encumbered by the stationery microphone and proceeded to create fresh, new problems for themselves. Maybe they had been watching too much Oral Roberts on television. Or maybe they wanted both fists free to pound the pulpit. Whatever the reason, they sought out more freedom of movement with the ever-popular "clip-on" microphone. This is one that attaches to the coat lapel or collar of the robe. And its ultimate purpose is apparently to amplify the rustle of clothes, the breathing of lungs, and the clearing of throats. And if this is true, then it does one heck of a good job. If this is true, then I've never seen one fail.

But all of this takes me back to the original sound system, the one I described with the tone knob and volume knob and a single on/off switch. Back to about 1958. I was 13 years old and our old brownstone church was just moving into the modern age. We had just bought new robes for the choir and a new organ with pedals. But most importantly, we had just bought our first sound system.

Mr. Parker, our minister, was a very proper man, as you would expect. He was over six feet tall, broad-chested (he did a hundred push-ups every morning), thin-waisted (he did a hundred sit-ups every morning), and was as bald as an apple. He was what you may think of when you think of a typical stiff-collared Presbyterian minister. A good man, but still a Presbyterian.

It was at the beginning of one of those summertime "song services." And to get the full understanding of what happened, you have to know exactly where our church was located. It was on the highway, but in the back, as the crow flies, about a half a mile through a cornfield and a cow pasture, there stood the transmitting tower to our local radio station. Although this had never been a problem before and as far as I know, since, on this particular August night the stars must have been aligned or the humidity must have been just right or an ill wind must have been blowing at just the most opportune slant, because at exactly the right moment, the wrong thing happened.

We had just finished singing the opening hymn and because some unthinking deacon had failed to turn on the microphone, Mr. Parker in his pure white summer suit (he really was a sharp dresser) said, "Let's bow our heads in prayer," and realizing the amp was not yet turned on reached down and hit the on switch. And as he did, the entire church was filled with "HELLO, BABY. THIS IS THE BIG BOP-PER SPEAKING."

Parker's scrambling and our laughing spoiled any chance for a religious experience that night. It was explained later that the radio station was playing "Chantilly Lace," the number one song in the nation at that time, at just that precise moment and the amplifier under the pulpit was in a perfect line to pick up the signal and broadcast it in the church like a Motorola floor model. I've thought on this moment many times through the years, as every word of it is true, and I've tried to think what I would change to make it a funnier story. Is there another song that would work better? Another line from that song? Another preacher with another look on his face? And the answer always comes up the same.

You can't mess with the truth and you can't mess with a sound system in church or the Big Bopper will get you.

TURN YOUR RADIO ON,
AND LISTEN TO THE MUSIC IN THE AIR.
TURN YOUR RADIO ON,
HEAVEN'S GLORY SHARE.
TURN THE LIGHTS DOWN LOW,
AND LISTEN TO THE MASTER'S RADIO.
GET IN TOUCH WITH GOD,
TURN YOUR RADIO ON.

Softball

Softball was a big deal at our church when I was growing up. Everybody played. We had a Junior League that was the training ground, the stepping-stone, the farm team for our adult league. The Junior League played maybe eight or ten games a summer, but what was most fun were the practices. I loved, when I was 10, 11, 12 years old, knowing that I had ball practice at the diamond behind the church at 3 p.m. Thursday afternoon or

10 a.m. Saturday morning. It was the highlight of my week. I lived for it.

Correction. What I lived for was being old enough, 13, if I remember correctly, to play on the adult team. I got my uniform at 13 but little else. I didn't see much field time, but who cared. I had the bright green uniform, the socks and stirrups, the cap, and the jacket. We always had a good team. All my friends and all my brother's friends were good ballplayers and it was fun even when we didn't win, which was seldom.

There were eight local churches involved who supported it financially, so we had a pretty nice facility that just happened to be on our church property. We had a concession stand and lights and even a microphone and loudspeaker. We were big time. But with all this we had rules. And they were expected to be honored.

The most severe one was church attendance. If you didn't come and pray, you couldn't come and play. Every team player had to attend church at least two Sundays a month during the season, which ran from May through August. And the church fathers kept a pretty watchful eye and tight rein on it. The result of this was overflowing pews in the spring and summer. Teenagers you'd never see till the lilies bloomed again next year would rush the front doors for that 10 o'clock service and the Sunday school hour that followed so they could officially be counted present and included in Monday night's lineup.

Looking back, it was a pretty good incentive to get the youth to church.

The best softball story to come from all this sports/church history came from the generation just ahead of me. The older guys who dominated the team just before my generation took over were very, very good. And I don't mean that casually. They, and there are still a few of them in the congregation today well into their seventies, were so good that one year they won practically every game on the schedule. I was only seven years into my life, but I remember the story vaguely as it unfolded and have relished in its retelling many times since.

They entered a state-wide tournament that year and wiped out every team in sight. They were hot. I can well recall the swirl of excitement over the fact that if they kept winning, they could possibly go to the "State." Hey, our little old church team just might get a chance to be in the state competition and just might get a chance to be the State Champions. The best church league team in Virginia. We couldn't be there in body but we were there in spirit and were glued to the radio and newspaper for the outcome. And, sure enough, the word came by phone late one evening that we had just won every game we played and the next game would put us in the State Championship in Richmond. I have no idea how many teams were involved but it was at least a three-day affair that none of my family traveled that far to see. But we certainly heard about it, as it became the shot from the bat heard round the church for years.

133

The tournament began on a hot Friday morning and you played till you dropped. Whoever was left standing went into Saturday and that's when it happened. Saturday evening the call came back to one of the elders of the church that our team had beaten every opponent they faced and was now one of two. And these two would play for the State Championship . . . Sunday afternoon at 3 p.m.

You have to realize this was 1952 in the South. You didn't go to movies on Sunday. You didn't play cards on Sunday, not even Animal Rummy. And you did not play ball on Sunday. And certainly not a Presbyterian church team on a Sunday afternoon. An immediate, emergency meeting of the session, the ruling body of our church, was called yet on Saturday night and it was decided that a telegram was to be sent to the team and its manager, all who were good-standing members of our congregation, (at least during ball season) telling them *not* to play ball on Sunday and further telling them to come home immediately.

Now the story switches to the other side. The ball team gets the telegram late Saturday night and they read it in silence. These were not teenagers. These were grown men who had just played their hearts out all summer and gotten as far as an amateur softball team could get. They were seven innings away from having it all. They sat a long time in silence looking at one another and then back at the telegram and then to their manager and finally someone spoke and for the life of me I've never been able to find out who, but someone said, "Let's tell them we never got the telegram."

Someone else said, "We can't do that. They'll never believe it."

Mr. Biby, the coach, was torn. He didn't want to go against the wishes of the church, but he also had 14 trophy-hungry ballplayers on his hands. The decision was obvious. He decided to take a vote.

And that's what they did. They took a vote and to no one's surprise it was unanimous; 14 – 0 to play the game. And when they got home they told the session they had voted and had played and there were some happy people and some very angry people. I don't know who was mad at whom. I've never been able to get a straight story about that. But the ball season was over for that year and things were said but I'm not sure by whom and I'm not sure to whom. The only thing I'm sure of is that today, as I write this, there is, standing on a high shelf in a prominent place in the library of our old time-healed church of one God, a large, slightly wounded trophy engraved with the words: 1952 STATE CHAMPIONS.

For 50 years it was lost and no one seemed to know whatever became of it. Some thought it was packed away in the church basement with other relics and trophies. Some thought it was never on the church grounds and should never be allowed on the church grounds. Others thought one of the old players might have it at his home. Some thought it was destroyed and

135

never made it home from Richmond. No one really knew until a renewed interest in the legend and the truth aroused the curiosity of someone not old enough to have known the facts when it all took place back in '52. And then it's amazing what a little snooping and probing will do.

So, as I said, it's on a shelf there in the church now, right or wrong. To quote Abe Lincoln, "You can't please all the Pharisees all the time."

Whoa! Was that Abe Lincoln that said that or was that me?

SO I'LL CHERISH THE OLD RUGGED CROSS,
TILL MY TROPHIES AT LAST I LAY DOWN.
I WILL CLING TO THE OLD RUGGED CROSS,
AND EXCHANGE IT SOMEDAY FOR A CROWN.

Sunday Movies

I have already told you what a mess it was when the church softball team played a game on Sunday. I've already explained that this was the South in the fifties and this sort of thing just didn't happen. Not among good church-going people like stiff-necked Presbyterians or hard-shelled Baptists. (My father-in-law told me one time that he had often been called a hard-shelled Baptist in derogatory tones, but that he had always considered it a compliment.)

There was nothing open on Sundays. No stores of any kind. No grocery stores. No department stores. No hardware stores. And drugstores? Let me tell you about that. There were about four drugstores in town and they used to take turns staying open on Sunday afternoons for emergencies. They worked together and coordinated their schedules with their competitors so the public would be served but so would the Sabbath.

Few people as possible worked on Sunday. My daddy did because he worked at a factory. And our minister, Mr. Lowman, who was a good friend of the family, used to tell Daddy it was okay to work on Sunday if you made an effort to use your weekday off as a day of rest and personal worship. Good advice, but I don't know if it was ever followed. (While we're talking about Lowman, Daddy told him, even after he started getting Sundays off, that the reason he still didn't come to church regularly was because he worked till midnight on Saturdays and when he came to church he often fell asleep during the sermon. Mr. Lowman, knowing my daddy to be the character he was, said, "That's okay, Sidney. I don't mind you sleeping through the sermon. At least that way I know where you are.")

So when the theaters started opening on Sunday afternoons in the mid-fifties, it was a big, big deal. It was forbidden. Tolerated by few. And forgiven by even fewer. My friend, Bobby, broke the ice with his first Sunday movie by going to see *The Robe,* starring Richard Burton and Jean Simmons. It was about the crucifixion. He sold his mother on the fact that because it was a biblical movie, it would be alright. The real reason he wanted to go was because it was the first Cinemascope movie ever made and he wanted to see what that was all about. He went and told me all about it and to this day I have still never seen *The Robe.* Maybe I'll catch it on TV sometime yet.

I don't remember my first one, but my favorite Sunday movie story has to do with my older brother Harold and his best friend Phil. Teenagers, they each had dates one Sunday night and for some reason, instead of double dating, they decided to go their separate ways. Harold and his date, for the lack of somewhere to light, wound up at the drive-in. His first movie on the Lord's Day of rest. He took the girl home afterward and said he had that hollow feeling in his stomach that you have when you skip school. You know you have done something wrong and it eats away at your conscience like the sun after a popsicle.

Now as all teenage boys do (just ask if you don't believe me), Harold and Phil met up after they took their respective dates home, and sat around and talked. He finally told Phil, "You'll never guess what I did tonight. I went to the movies."

Phil listened intently to his confession and began to laugh. He said, "So did I."

Two young Presbyterian boys stepping out of the box at the same time and neither one of them knowing what the other one was doing.

I've asked them about this story lately. They remember the night distinctly and clearly. It was the summer of 1956 and Harold went to the Skyline Drive-In to see *The Flesh and the Spur,* starring John Agar. Phil went to the Dixie to see *Hollywood or Bust* with Dean Martin and Jerry Lewis.

They both remember the year, the movie, and the night. But neither one can recall the girl.

Sometimes the guilt outlasts the pleasure.

JESUS KNOWS ALL ABOUT OUR STRUGGLES;
HE WILL GUIDE TILL THE DAY IS DONE.
THERE'S NOT A FRIEND LIKE THE LOWLY JESUS,
NO NOT ONE! NO NOT ONE!

Sunday School

Sunday school just may be the most useful tool in the Christian church. When I was a kid, it kept me interested in going to church. The sermons were over my head. But Sunday school was tailor made for each individual age group.

In the kindergarten department, we got the standard one-sheet color picture with the simple Bible story printed on the back. A couple of years later you'd get promoted to the primary department and get the same Bible stories but with a little more detail. The juniors would hear the same old, old story again, but this time with a little history and a little more meaning. And by the time you got to the senior group, the high school age, there was discussion and plenty of it, because all teenagers from the age of about 14 up suddenly become aware that they know everything about anything and are not shy in sharing their opinions. I have always had plenty of opinion to share, even when I was short on facts.

Then came the adult classes, and those same wonderful old stories are now read and viewed from an entirely different angle. John Wayne once said in an interview when asked about the rating system on movies, that in the golden age of movies they did a scene and the kids got one thing from it and the adults something else. And that's exactly how the Bible is written. Those Sunday classes were not so much set up on ages as they were on perspectives. Today I still look forward to that hour after the morning worship service to get with folks who are as eager as me to learn and discuss and share.

Did you notice I said "that hour after the morning worship"? In our church, we have the worship service first and *then* Sunday school. I know of few other churches that do it in this order, but you may find it interesting as to why we do. And then you may not, but here it is anyway.

Years ago, back in the 1930s, before I was even a thought in anyone's mind, we shared a minister with another church.

And in order for him to deliver both sermons, one church had to switch their morning schedule around. Straws, I suppose, were drawn, and we lost. He would preach at 10 a.m. at our church, leave during the last hymn, speed across the county to the second church, arrive during their first hymn, and preach to them during the 11 o'clock hour. After a few years of this, when we finally got our own minister, we just never bothered to change back. So I grew up with this order and it seems right to me.

Now on the other hand, my wife, Debbie, grew up in a church, Primitive Baptist, that had no Sunday school at all. It's just the nature of that particular denomination. I have asked and researched as to the why, and all I can glean from the answers I get is that they wanted the gospel preached and stated and not dissected and discussed. And to their credit, people do sometimes tend to fall out over discussing (discussing leads to arguing) the Bible. So this was her background and she never attended a Sunday school class until we were married and she joined the local Southern Baptist church.

After a short while, being a schoolteacher for years when she was younger, the deacons in her church recognized her flare and talent and approached her to take over teaching an adult Sunday morning class. She flatly refused them. But after two or three invitations, she discussed it with me and I encouraged her and she took the leap and now co-teaches the largest class in her church.

143

The punch line here is this. Once she agreed to teach, I said to her, "Be sure to call your mom and daddy and tell them. They'll really be proud of you."

Her reply was, "I don't want them to know what I'm doing. They might not approve."

I had to laugh out loud. Of all the things we all have done in our lives that we didn't want our mamas and daddies to know about, teaching Sunday school was not something I would have ever thought about keeping from them.

In time, she told them and all was well. But it puts in light just what an important step this was. Those who teach should never take it lightly and those who appoint the teachers should never do it randomly. Young minds and serious subjects are at hand. Mature minds and sundry opinions are at risk. Jesus even warns us in Matthew that we are in danger if we teach the wrong things. It can't get much plainer than that.

Sunday school is the dessert of Sunday morning worship. A little lighter than the sermon. A little fluffier than hell fire and brimstone. A little more social than being preached to. And a little easier to swallow when you can talk back and ask questions and get involved. More people ought to try it. Besides, we always have coffee and sticky buns.

144

MORE ABOUT JESUS LET ME LEARN,
MORE OF HIS HOLY WILL DISCERN;
SPIRIT OF GOD, MY TEACHER BE,
SHOWING THE THINGS OF CHRIST FOR ME.

MORE, MORE ABOUT JESUS,
MORE, MORE ABOUT JESUS,
MORE OF HIS SAVING FULLNESS SEE,
MORE OF HIS LOVE WHO DIED FOR ME.

Vacation Bible School

Every summer, in the hottest part of June, we would have vacation Bible school. It was for kids from birth to 12 years old, and I looked forward to it from one year to the next. We'd have a Bible class, a craft class, and, best of all, a recess, which would take us outside to the softball diamond behind the church and to my favorite summer pastime.

We would convene at 9 a.m., Monday through Friday for two weeks, and disperse at noon. There were always cookies and Kool-Aid — grape, cherry, or orange. Always Bible verses to memorize. And always things that we had made to carry home at the end of the two weeks.

The summer I was ten I memorized the 1st and 100th Psalms, took a firm disliking to orange Kool-Aid, and wove a lanyard. The lanyard, it seems, sticks more prominently in my mind, although I just realized as I paused from writing these very words, that I can still recite both Psalms. But back to the craft at hand. Let me admit right here that until that summer of my life, I had never heard of a lanyard and had no idea what one was or looked like or was used for. And to be completely honest with you, I have never really heard of one since. So just in case you're a little fuzzy yourself on what a lanyard is, let me explain.

You have three strands of thin plastic, one white, one navy blue, and one sky blue, and you weave them around and into one another until you have a large loop with a tail on it. This cord-like necklace then is woven around a silver hook and you have a lanyard. And what's it good for you may ask? To hang your whistle on, of course. What else?

That was the big craft of the summer of my tenth year. The Psalms, the Kool-Aid, and the lanyard. And I loved everything about Bible school — the teachers, the other kids in my class, and, as I mentioned before, the softball.

But of all the memories and teachings that I still hold on to from that summer, there is one life-lesson that I learned that I am reminded of everyday of my life and I really didn't learn it at Bible School. I learned it in leaving Bible School and I cherish it to this very day.

As I have told you earlier, noon was when the classes let out, and I, along with a few of the other guys, would head directly to the softball diamond on our bikes with our gloves hooked on to the handlebars and the equipment bag that always stayed there at the church, and ready ourselves for an afternoon of shagging flies and running bases. But on this one day, I was late leaving the classroom for some reason now lost to the ages, and by the time I got outside, none of my friends were in sight. So I mounted my old, beat up 24-inch and headed down the hill toward the diamond. But when I got there I stopped short and stood with my bike between my legs and stared at a sight I had never seen before. There on our church diamond were about a dozen black kids, my age and older, playing ball. (Let me insert right here that at the time they were "colored." If you had called any one of them "black" then, you would have had a fight on your hands.)

I watched them play for a few minutes and listened to them laugh and tease one another. They seemed to genuinely be having a good time, not unlike my friends and myself on any other given afternoon. I never said anything to them and they never said anything to me and I think I felt some sort of fear in being the only "white boy" there. So I left.

And fear is not really the right word. I just felt alone and out of place. Different. Displaced. I turned my bike around and headed home, which was all of five minutes away. I pulled in the driveway, kicked the kickstand down, and went in the kitchen and got a Pepsi out of the refrigerator and was sitting at the kitchen table drinking and daydreaming when Mama walked into the room.

She said, "What are you doing home so early? I thought you were going to play ball this afternoon."

I said, "I was. But when I got to the diamond, there were a whole bunch of colored kids already there."

And what she said to me next, molded my outlook, my heart, and my life. She said, "So? Don't they know how to play ball?"

Just that simple. That's how she was and is. A lesson with few words. I never finished that Pepsi. I went outside and got back on my bike and headed back to the ball field and I never came home till suppertime. And she was right. They did know how to play ball!

Some of our best-learned lessons are not from books or from the classroom or from trained teachers. Some of our best learned-lessons are from the heart. And my mother has the best one in the world.

JUST AS I AM! THO TOSSED ABOUT,
WITH MANY A CONFLICT, MANY A DOUBT.
FIGHTING AND FEARS WITHIN, WITHOUT,
O LAMB OF GOD! I COME! I COME!

Visitation

I t was summertime, just after suppertime, and I saw them coming up the front walk. I recognized them as two men from church. I ran back through the house calling my mother and telling her two men were at the front door. Mr. Wade and Mr. Young. And the reason they were there was that it was visitation season. The elders and the deacons teamed up two-by-two, just the way Jesus sent them out, and visited everyone in the church.

As a rule, they didn't stay long. They just sat and talked and asked if everything was okay at church. Sort of fishing around, I think, for any problems. We had none, and pretty soon they were on their way to the next congregant in their quest for the every-member canvass. I watched them go and thought, even at that young age, just how awkward and uncomfortable a situation it was for them to go into every member's home and make conversation and fish for potential problems and then have a prayer and leave. Probably 20 other pairs were out there doing the same thing that night. Then next week they'd all get together in one of the Sunday school rooms and compare notes and see what they had to work on.

Many years later, I was one of those elders. Then I learned the real reasons for those visits. My family was visited for just the reason I suspected, but also to seek out pledges for the building fund. Other families were dropped in on because they didn't attend church regularly. This was just a little nudge visit. Some families got the knock on the door to find out if they were *ever* coming back so they would know whether to take them off the church roll or not. Presbyterians have to pay a fee for every member carried on the official roll. We don't want to purge anyone too soon, but we also don't want any dead weight that may be costing us a buck.

We don't visit much anymore. Maybe it's because the building program is complete. Or maybe because there are no particular problems to solve. Or maybe it's just because it's a different time. Folks don't like drop-ins today even if it is church business. And you know what? This suits me just fine because I never wanted to be on that visiting end anyway. I wouldn't know what to say. I'd feel like the unwanted telemarketer who gets hung up on during the dinner hour. After ringing the doorbell three times and having no one answer, I'd get to thinking the whole family is probably hiding in a closet waiting for us to make our descent off the porch. And Jesus even allowed for this. He told his 12 to spread the Word, but if they weren't welcomed, to shake the dust off their feet and leave. I'd probably be shaking the dust before I rang the bell.

I'm a good disciple, but not always a real good apostle. Not nearly as good as those men who came to visit us when I was a kid.

But I'll keep trying.

> SOWING IN THE MORNING,
> SOWING SEEDS OF KINDNESS,
> SOWING IN THE NOONTIDE
> AND THE DEWY EVE;
> WAITING FOR THE HARVEST,
> AND THE TIME OF REAPING,
> WE SHALL COME REJOICING,
> BRINGING IN THE SHEAVES.

BRINGING IN THE SHEAVES,
BRINGING IN THE SHEAVES,
WE SHALL COME REJOICING,
BRINGING IN THE SHEAVES.
BRINGING IN THE SHEAVES,
BRINGING IN THE SHEAVES,
WE SHALL COME REJOICING,
BRINGING IN THE SHEAVES.

Weddings

Every young woman wants at least one big church wedding, snow-white gown with flowing train and lace about the neck. Prince Charming on her right, her girl-friends on her left, a ring on her finger and bells on her toes. A borrowed blue garter from an errant aunt and a sanctuary full of family and friends to witness every move. It's her big day. It's showtime and the bride is the star of the show. She gets to dress up at her prettiest, invite all of her extended family and envious friends, and walk down the center aisle with dramatic strands of music swelling from the organ. Amid smiles and tears aplenty, she meets the love of her life at the altar and proclaims her undying devotion in front of all the world. What young woman doesn't want to live this fairy tale?

I've seen many through the years in our medium-sized church. Some took and some didn't. Some lasted longer than expected and some were over before the flowers died. And just about any church can claim this same ratio of success and failure. The preacher does his best. The organist plays what's requested and the soloist sings some pop piece that is professed to be "their song." The mothers of the bride and groom cry, the fathers look scared and bored, and the groom is standing there in fear of what his friends are going to do to his car. Rented tuxedos and pastel dresses are the order of the day and after the official pictures are taken and the last piece of cake eaten, the fairy tale ends and life begins, and may God bless us all.

Many are heard to comment on how beautiful the church looks and what lovely flowers they are and we're all very happy the honored couple decided to exchange their vows in our humble little bethel, but all the time knowing that more likely than not, the bride and groom will never darken the door of the church again until their firstborn is baptized. But then there are a few who do and this is how we grow. This feeds the Sunday school system and the collection plate and the spiritual needs of a family that will keep life in the old building until their kids come along and walk the same center aisle to the same strands of Mendelssohn.

And then there's the reception. Thank heavens we have a wonderful kitchen and fellowship hall to accommodate reasonable crowds, but that's not the point. The point is the elaborateness of it all. When was the last time you were at a wedding reception and they only served cake and punch? Probably in another century. (I like saying that, even though the phrase has lost its significance recently.) How about decades ago? Now it has to be a major catering event. Often a sit-down meal, and if not that at least fancy finger foods I can't pronounce. But in spite of it all, a wedding is a beautiful thing. A happy and joyous occasion that leaves sweet and wonderful memories in the air that come flooding back on any given Sunday morning, bringing a smile to even the most cynical face.

On the other hand, and you didn't think I was going to leave it at that did you? On the other hand, the most memorable wedding I ever attended, and I'm not sure now why I was even there, I saw at least two pair of sandals, a pair of shorts, and a golf shirt in the pew beside me. And when the groom entered, some crony in the back yelled, "Go for it, Ed!"

I'm proud to say this wasn't in our church, but you know what? Ed and his bride are just as married as me and mine or you and yours. As long as God is in it, no one else can spoil it.

LITTLE IS MUCH WHEN GOD IS IT!
LABOR NOT FOR WEALTH OR FAME.
THERE'S A CROWN AND YOU CAN WIN IT,
IF YOU GO IN JESUS' NAME.

The Church

I have talked about nearly every aspect of the church one can think of. All the services and the sacraments and the social life. But I'd be remiss if I didn't spend a few minutes on the church itself.

Let's start with the building. The first one I knew was an old brownstone with a rope hanging in the vestibule that was connected to the bell in the steeple tower. The pews were dark wood and they curved to form a coziness throughout the entire sanctuary that made you feel you were in a much smaller and warmer area. I was baptized there, married there, and sang in the choir there. Then it was razed for a new highway and we went back about a hundred yards and built a new one. This one didn't have the dark, curved pews, but it had the bellpull in the narthex and I used to hold my sons up when they were little and let them ring the bell on Sunday mornings. It doesn't have the style the old church had, but it has the same people and that's what makes it home.

And I often think of those people who don't know what a "church family" is. You and I both know people who have no church at all. We know folks who say they don't need to go to church to be a Christian. And you know what? They're right. But I always figured if you were a Christian you'd *want* to go to church. But some of these folks say they can stay home and watch any number of television preachers on Sunday morning and get all they need to save their souls. And again, they're right. And there's no way you can tell them anything different.

But what they don't know they're missing is the church itself. The building and the people. The "church family" and a place to come to and meet and share in a mutual emotion that can be replaced by nothing else in this tired old world of ours. People to pray with and talk to. People to help and people to help you. People who care when you're sick and worried. People who need you. People who fill baskets at Thanksgiving and teach little kids Bible stories about David and Paul. People who sing together and hold each other's hand when only the touch or hug of another human being can say what words can't. People who visit the sick and wait at the hospital with the family when all hope is gone.

This is what Sunday mornings are all about. And every one of them is a memory I can't live without.

O I'D LIKE TO GO BACK
TO THAT OLD COUNTRY CHURCH,
TO HEAR THE SONGS OF PRAISE.
HOW THE PEOPLE WOULD SING;
IT WOULD MAKE THE RAFTERS RING
AT THAT OLD COUNTRY CHURCH.

Epilogue

Looking back and taking stock
        of all I've done and seen,
My favorite times always seem
        to be the childhood scenes.
Maybe they were wonderful
        and something to behold,
Or maybe they've gotten better
        as I have gotten old.

Could it be I really felt
        the things I thought I did?
Or is that simply me today,
        searching for that kid?
If I were sworn to tell the truth
        and held to take an oath,
I'm afraid I'd find that it would be,
        a little bit of both.

But every word and every thought
        that I have shared with you
Have brought me close to tears because
        I know them to be true
'Cause if you mix together,
        Time and Love in equal part,
It can serve up a Memory
        that's too big for the heart.

Maybe it was the singing,
          or the songs they would choose
Or the preacher in the pulpit,
          or the people in the pews
Or maybe it was Mama,
          or just the hand I was dealt,
Or maybe it was simply,
          the hand of God I felt.

Every part played a part
          in who I am today,
The way I think, the way I act,
          the things I do and say
And of all the precious minutes past
          I can't recall, and yet,
Those Sunday Morning Memories
          are some I can't forget.

An original member of the Statler Brothers, country music's premier singing group for nearly 40 years, Don Reid has written over 200 published and recorded songs. He has received numerous awards and accolades worldwide for his singing and songwriting, and even co-wrote seven seasons of the number one variety series, "The Statler Brothers Show."

Don is the father of two sons, Debo and Langdon, and he lives in his hometown of Staunton, Virginia, with his wife, Deborah. He is an elder and Sunday school teacher in the Presbyterian church where he has been a member since childhood.

Also by Don Reid

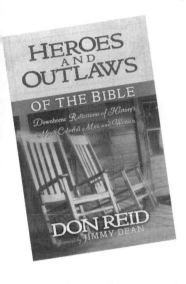

HEROES AND OUTLAWS OF THE BIBLE

DOWNHOME REFLECTIONS OF HISTORY'S MOST COLORFUL MEN AND WOMEN

Utilizing the same talent that penned some of country music's most-loved hits, Don Reid reflects on the lives of the great-yet-simple men and women of the Bible. Abraham, Joseph, Esther, and John the Baptist are some of the people included. With a gift for telling a story in a factual, folksy manner, he points out the successes that made these people great, while also describing the weaknesses that made them human. This down-to-earth, amusing book lets us see a little bit of ourselves in the lives of these men and women — and when you get down to it, they were not super-humans; they were just folks like you and me.

ISBN: 0-89221-531-3 • 168 pages • casebound • $13.99

Available in Christian bookstores nationwide